WIZ

MW01538583

THE MAGICK, WITCHCRAFT & CEREMONIAL ARTS OF MERLYN STONE

Edited by Joshua Free
Preface by James Thomas
With Foreword by Myrddin Wolfe

*Originally published by Joshua Free in 1998
under the pseudonym of "Merlyn Stone" as
"The Sorcerer's Handbook", now coupled with
"The Lost Books of Merlyn Stone."*

© 2011, Joshua Free

No part of this publication may be reproduced in any form or by any means, electronic or mechanical, including photocopying, recording, or by any information storage or retrieval system, without permission in writing from the publisher.

BOOK ONE:
THE SORCERER'S HANDBOOK
OF MERLYN STONE

BOOK TWO:
THE LOST BOOKS OF MERLYN STONE

MARDUKITE

PREFACE

What has the "New Age," the age of "enlight-enment" become? Where is the true enlighten-ment? Where are the "no-nonsense" books for those who wish to live a mystical life of self-honest enchanted enlightenment? Even the *New Age* has become blind and led astray from its true purpose. Much of the work of the noble wizard has become the "work" of fools seeking power, curses, and other things that will get you no where spiritually. Many well known new age authors now *"fluff up"* their newest release to appeal to the lonely house wife, the disturbed teenager, and many others who would use these things as a way to fix their problems, but not receive any enlightenment in the process. They see what many call "magick" as a way to make their lives easier so they don't have to do the work, and the problem is so many of these books advertise themselves in that way! Where is the enlightenment, where is the self honesty, where is the *true magick?*

Being a young adult myself, I know the feeling of searching for something more. After a year or two of being involved in the *New Age*, I was already noticing these things in the latest releases and I was only 13 at the time! I had always been drawn to two things in the new age. First was the *"Necronomicon"* (any of them) and second the the name "Merlin" or "Merlyn" in any book title. This is what led me to Joshua Free's book, *"Merlyn's Magick: The Wizards Secret Notebooks."* I was around 15 at this point in which I ordered the book.

When I first opened the book, I had no idea what to expect. By the time I had finished the book, I was shocked. There was no "fluff," *no sparkles and rainbows*. This was true enlightenment! Something I had really only felt a few times before when reading books by "Simon" and Douglas Monroe.

There was no nonsense here; only the feeling of true, down-to-the-bone magick and wisdom. After watching some of the author's *"How to Be A Wizard"* video series on *youtube*, I began to research him more. Then, imagine my excitement when in the summer of 2009, when I found his new translation of the *"Necronomicon"* on eBay and after sending him a message over myspace, he responded, back to me that very same night! I believe my exact words were: "A new age author who actually responds to his fans!" This started a friendship between us.

The above paragraph was not off topic. You see, I had not known before talking with Joshua that he wrote most of "*Merlyns Magick*" as a teenager. I found this out after we began corresponding over the internet. I was in awe, that a teenager could have written this masterpiece. The works were written from ages 11 to 16! Being around 17 at the time, I thought that was the coolest thing in the world! Eventually he re-released some of the *Merlyn Stone* books in handmade copies and then in bound book form later on. I bought every single one. Now: was this work as "groundbreaking" as the current Mardukite work? *Probably not*, but it set the foundations for the author, and many others to build upon.

These books started something that Joshua has followed ever since. A call to find the truth. A call to enlighten those who would listen. Of course what really started his writing happened thousands of years ago, but that's another story. (One well worth reading might I add! *"Nabu Speaks!"*) For this life though, these books were the foundation. You can't ascend the pyramid unless you start at the beginning and work your way up.

So it is with great pleasure that I write these words, this *introduction*, if you will, for the re-release of the complete anthology of *Merlyn Stone* works. These works have really broken the barriers and are presented in a way that will delight all those who read them.

Remember all those questions from the start of this introduction? Well what you are about to read and learn are the *answers!* Where is the *real magick?* Where is the work of the *noble wizard?* Where is the book for those who search for *real mystical enlightenment?* It is here! In your hands!

May your journey be bright and blessed, and may the Anunnaki guide you on your path.

~ James Thomas
Mardukite Admin
Autumn Equinox, 2011

MARDUKITE

FOREWORD

Sorcery. The very word conjures images of all things magick – from the classic Merlin, to today's modern stage magicians. In the depths of our imagination, magick and sorcery have always fascinated the human race. Is it any wonder that here at the end of the 20th century our society turns back toward all things magickal?

I began my magickal education while attending college. Little then did I realize, so was a young boy who would later write the volume you now hold. My first brush with the enigmatic Merlyn Stone came almost a decade after I began my own magickal career. Looking through a catalog one day I spotted the ad for his debut work, *The Sorcerer's Handbook*. The ad spoke about how the book "told it all without all the usual occult jargon." That was its biggest selling point for me, so I bought it.

I was pleasantly surprised when my copy arrived. Not only did it fulfill my expectations – it surpassed them. *The Sorcerer's Handbook* presented many facets of occult knowledge in plain, easy to understand, language. Best of all though, it made magick practical for even the newest student.

I was, however, in for one more little surprise. *Merlyn Stone*, it seemed, was only a high school student when he wrote the book I held. I was floored! How could a mere teenager understand this much of the occult, much less write a book about it? Luckily, I got the chance to ask him about it! He had included his web address and email address in the book – and being ever so curious, I wrote him. I had to know how some-one so young could pull this off. That's when I was able to discover just what type of person Merlyn Stone really is.

Although young in body, he is quite mature in mind beyond description – someone who modern magick practitioners would call an "old soul." He represents a new breed of magician – someone who dares, no matter the odds.

This volume you hold represents a milestone of achievement – a revised an expanded edition of *The Sorcerer's Handbook* that is enhanced with clarifications drawn from his other works. This book is the pinnacle of all things magickal and practical – a beacon to shed new light on magick: the light of practicality.

And may it shine throughout the new millennium.

Enjoy it and happy reading!

~ Myrddin Wolfe
November 1999

INTRODUCTION TO THE 1998 EDITION

I gaze at the bookshelf before me and wonder what the New Age has really accomplished. I see an annotated 1000-page edition of Agrippa's *Occult Philosophy*, the Kabbalists *Sefer Yetzirah* and a million words comprising theosophy's *Secret Doctrine*, not to mention the bulk of materials composing a *Complete System of Golden Dawn Magic* and volume upon volume by Aleister Crowley and Kenneth Grant. . .

Man has certainly been engulfed with information in his "age of enlightenment," but what practical work comes from all this knowledge? What I have accomplished alone and with the assistance of others in my short life thus far has already superseded those who have been content in only knowing the magickal theories and the concepts of metaphysics. These "bookshelf sorcerer's" have never *known* magick – never felt its power running through their veins. They were content to just talk about it. . .*and I was not*.

Magick is NOT a bi-monthly newsletter, a fancy society or organization or a weekly class.

15

It is life itself and all that makes up existence. Every person in this world faces the building blocks of magick each day. The *"sorcerer"* (a term chosen for the operators of the present text of either gender) attains an upper hand because they can recognize the patterns and acknowledge these facets as they truly are, using them to manifest the world desired.

The *"sorcerer"* seeks to unlock the *secrets* of the Universe, questioning the human-fashioned truths of the world and to transcend the animalistic nature of *homo ferox* [editor's note: literally *"man, the ferocious"* – from T.H. White's *"Book of Merlyn"*]. The sorcerer can essentially do and become anything – it this removal of trust and attention from abstract deities and concepts, placing it rightful within "self" that causes such a being to be the most powerful "system" functioning on the planet. . . *and potentially the most dangerous.*

Behind the scenes it has been *"us,"* the *"sorcerers"* that make the "world go 'round." Since the dawn of time, the astrologers, magi and priestly wizards have been the true *"Guardians"* of the Earth. The Sumerians, Egyptians and Greeks of the ancient times all give evidence of this by their spiritual traditions. We look at it today and call it myth, but it was certainly not so to them. Two-thousand years from now, historians may very well look at our present world in a different light.

Who has read the *Old Testament* and not noticed the tremendous magickal powers of Moses? And also of the mystics who aided the Pharaoh...? And was it not by occult sciences that the "wise men" were led to the Christ-child? And what of the occult mysteries embedded in the religious ceremonial transformation of water into wine? True alchemy or a fabrication? And yet still today, the orthodox religions have forbidden the "*lay person*" from practicing the birth-right of magick!

Magick is a friend who seeks embrace, not fear. It is the girl-friend (or boy-friend) who is always there when you wake up in the morning and always returns your *calls*. As they say: *to know her is to love her*. Magick need not be honored as a religion, but is validated by true religion: as the theosophists say: *there is no religion higher than truth*. The practice of magick requires purification, research and dedication, not worship.

~Merlyn Stone
1998

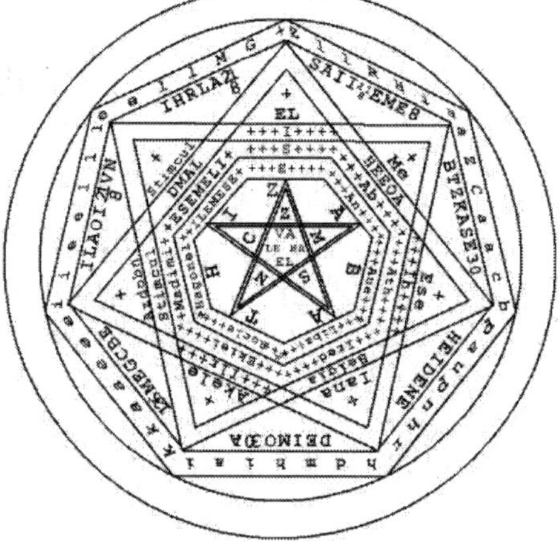

SORCERER'S
HANDBOOK
OF MERLYN STONE

MARDUKITE
CHAMBERLAINS

THE CORE OF MAGICK

ENERGY

It exists in all things and is likewise the driving force behind all magick. Whether something is living or not, it has energy, a force that can be changed and manipulated by the will of the "*sorcerer.*" Energy cannot cease to exist, nor can it be created. It simply *is*. But constantly is it revolving and abounding, changing form. The sorcerer is one who seeks to recognize the patterns and cause them to change in accordance with their will.

All the actions, words, symbols and dramatic enactments performed in ritual magick are meaningless without the proper currents of energy. The energy required for magick is everywhere around us, although invisible to the untrained eye. The sorcerer therefore learns to recognize this energy, to channel and harvest it for personal gain. More than a special religion or cult-following, "magick" is a way in which to view the world and interpret life.

There are two main sources of energy that are

utilized in magick. Firstly, there is personal power, the energy that enables one to walk, sleep, study, think. . .and have sex. This energy can be raised for magickal purposes through mental concentration and the tensing of the physical muscles in the body. It can be directed in currents (rays) to any source to more easily create change on a mundane level.

The second source of energy is external. Very often in lower magick and earth-oriented systems, this second source is *Nature-power*. In high and ceremonial forms of magick, this power may come from the astral plane, the current of a spiritual deity (entity) or perhaps from another dimension or perceived level of reality. The powers of the *sorcerer* then are only limited by one's imagination – or more importantly, ones ability to visualize within imagination.

Through ritual magick, the *sorcerer* can raise personal power, merge it with external powers (which are called forth or summoned) and direct it with the "mind" via visualization. "*Visualization*," as we are told, "*is the key to the occult*."

MAGICK -vs- MAGIC

Aleister Crowley once said: "The whole question has been threshed out and organized by wise men of old; they have made a science of life complete and perfect; and they have given to it the name of MAGICK."

The primary means (numerology aside) for the change in spelling was to create a distinction between the practical occult magickal arts and the illusionist parlor tricks of magic by those who only *pretend* to manifest occult powers. Both spellings are accepted in the "New Age."

VISUALIZATION

A key to the process of magick is the "art" of visualization. This is the innate ability to create images and pictures in the mind. Problems on the physical plane are often created (and even resolved) from the process of "visualization". The mastery of visualization is a mental power which enables the sorcerer to gain a level of control over the physical world. Basic visualization-based rituals follows this formula:

1. raising energy

2. visualizing the change occurring
3. sending energy to the cause.

Thus is ritual magick, enabling one to allow changes to occur more rapidly then when left alone. In magickal terms, this is called the "channeling and harvesting of energy to direct it to a desired target to affect a change."

Visualization is the primary ability to maintain conscious control over the subconscious mind using innate faculties of "imagery." These skills allow you to observe changes as if they have already taken place and put attentive energies into these images. All change actually works on this principle: a person sees the desired change in their mind and then acts.

CEREMONIAL HIGH MAGICK

This style of magick is used by advanced sorcerers in order to manipulate the mental and spiritual planes. The magick energy discussed prior is sufficient for "manifesting" on the physical plane (in the mundane world). High magick delves deeper into the complexities of the systems, ceremonies and ritual aids used to represent abstract and spiritual concepts.

Magick using spellcraft, witchcraft and the like for purposes of affecting physical change is not "high magick." High Ceremonial Magick is used and mastered in order to bring about a state of transcendentalism, erupting from the belief that men can become more that the physical restrictions that the material systems portray. While the "New Age" has revived beliefs drawn from mystic folklore, cultural charms and spellcraft, the craft of wizards was also passed down a different stream.

Some traditions of "high magick" are also called "holy magick," noted for their particular alignment to the *"priestly"* systems of the "Great Work," accessed by methods not otherwise focused on the manipulation of the mundane world.

CONCENTRATION & THOUGHT DISCIPLINE

In addition to the ability to visualize concrete imagery, the sorcerer must also possess concentration and thought discipline. "Thought magick" requires the mental skills to hold a clear image in the mind for prolong periods of time. This is where most novices will usually require the most personal development to be able to execute effective magick.

Begin by sitting comfortably and allow your thoughts to drift for several minutes. First, go through what you were thinking and cause (or will) it to be replayed as precisely as possible. Next, allow your thoughts to drift and then still your mind, holding one thoughtform in your head for as long as you can. Don't strain, but focus on a single thought. If your mind begins to wander, gently correct yourself and begin to focus on the thought again. The final step is to keep the mind completely clear of all thoughts for as long as possible. Practice with these basic techniques is essential to gaining the necessary discipline over the mind.

Relaxation is critical to concentration. This is the ability to gain and keep a relaxed state of inner peace at will. Of course, not all magickal practices require a "sedated" state of mind, but absolute clarity in your focus is essential, including self-control and self-discipline, particularly concerning emotional energies. Such workings where violent imagery will better aid magick, would of course, be nullified by "relaxation" for the entire duration, but without proper focus, the energy in the ritual can become "wild magick."

Relaxation may be achieved by sitting or laying in a position comfortable and free of having to tense your muscles. When your muscles begin to tense or you get anxious, regulate your breathing and will your muscles to relax. Restlessness is fairly common to those who are not used to such stillness. Becoming proficient in such skills will greatly prepare you for the magickal work ahead.

As a final testament of your ability, try this: relax, clear your mind, then make an intentional recall of a specific recent event – consciously replaying the same stretch of information from memory, capturing as much of the original details as possible. Reproduce the emotional involvement and stimuli: visual, physical sensations, sounds, smells, and so forth.

Experiment further by "projecting" your ob-servational perspective into different aspects of the scene – see if you are able to examine a detail more closely than you had at the time of the event or perhaps you might recall an expression or reaction of someone else that you had noticed prior.

If you do not find blatant success with these techniques at first don't stress. Gently try at it some more as you continue your development further.

BREATHING

Rhythmic breathing is a prerequisite for most magickal work as part of the initial grounding process (not always indicated in an advanced ritual text). This simply becomes second nature to experienced practitioners. Proper breathing is not only important for your physical well-being, it also affects your ability to meditate, relax or energize your body (and aura).

During deliberate breathing, oxygen should be inhaled via the nose and exhaled through the mouth. Breathing solely in and out of the mouth is actually unhealthy because the air is not slowed and warmed through the sinuses.

Any mystical work involving energy (which is practically all of it) is enhanced through proper breathing – which distributes energy through the body. When you breathe in you can feel the energy flowing into your pores and flowing through the body.

28

By adding visualization imagery, you can project a conceptualized idea (or polarized energy) in the area around you and then interact with it (e.g. breathing it in or exhaling it into an environment).

Rhythmic breathing skills come from learning to gauge your breath. As you "count" specific intervals, your breath should be steady and maximized. Completely fill and empty your lungs, holding in between. This can be uncomfortable at first, but eventually it should yield a sensation of mild euphoria (as its amazing what proper breathing can do). One popular method we call "quad-breathing," counting four seconds or heartbeats for each part of the cycle: breathing in (counting to four), holding (counting to four), exhaling (counting. . .) and holding.

WILLPOWER

It is imperative for a sorcerer to maintain a true sense of self (in self-honesty). The sorcerer must always be in control of the body and mind – must always have control over the actions and thoughts that ensue from said body and mind. This is called true "willpower" or "self-direction."

Practice at this may require gaining a more awkward routine – pushing yourself to behave in a way you might not norm-ally do. That is to say: don't allow clocks, schedules and impuls-ive "desires" to rule your life. When hungry, tired or the like, wait a little while longer. See if you can manipulate these sensations or trans-form them into something else. This is not to say to deprive yourself, but learn to do more than "react," learn to actually "act". This type of training actually increases one's control over the body – after all, how can you transcend the physical body if you are bound by it?

MAGICKAL CORRESPONDENCES

LUNAR POWERS

The word "month" is semantically connected to the Moon's cycle. This can be measured in both "sidereal" or "synodic" periods. A sidereal month is approximately 27.3 days and marks the time for the moon to physically complete an orbit. The synodic month takes the perceived rotation/spin of the Earth into consideration and takes approximately 29.5 days. Together, these figures give us an "observed" lunar month of 28 days. Lunar calendars dating back to the Sumerians and Babylonians possess 29 and 30-day months.

Sorcerers have long felt that the moon has a significant impact on our lives and on the planet itself. Since magick is generally thought to be oriented toward "Nature" or the "Universe," the effect of the moon on mystical work has become a heavy influence in modern magickal traditions, as well as icons of the same – *a lunar goddess* – although the ancient Sumerian system gave the moon male attributes.

31

Magickal workings and performances can be gauged to the proper times of a lunar phase in order to add lunar energies to a ritual. Different lunar phases impact in different ways. Of course, it is not always possible for the sorcerer to wait for the proper lunar timing to do a magickal working.

The *Full Moon* is a "psychic high-tide." It is the strongest time for the invocational spells that draw or attract some-thing towards you. This could be love, protection, healing, etc. The *New Moon* is a time for darker workings – those workings, which are secret and hidden. A second new moon in a single month is called the *Dark Moon* and is thought to be even more powerful than a regular new moon. Likewise, the second full moon in a month is called the *Blue Moon*.

The *waxing moon* is a period between the new moon and the full, when the moon is perceived to be getting larger. Since the light is strength-ening it is a perfect time for invocational magick – that which draws something to you. A *waning moon* falls between the full moon and the new, when the moon is perceived to be getting smaller. Many view this as a time of purification and banishing.

PLANETARY POWERS

Planetary influences are a reoccurring theme in magickal notebooks and grimoires. Each day of the week is "ruled" by a specific celestial planet and these influences are coupled with lunar phases to gauge the timing for many spells and rituals of material interest. Many grimoires catalogue their hierarchy of spiritual entities by the governing planets, also correlating to favorable timing for making contact with them via ceremonial magick.

SUNDAY – Sun – Leadership, sacredness, success, power, God, solar observations, change and fire.

MONDAY – Moon – Faerie magick, psychic/ psionic development, Goddess and the water element.

TUESDAY – Mars – Courage, protection magick, military endeavors and victory.

WEDNESDAY – Mercury – Communication, mental, development, divination, intellect, air element.

THURSDAY – Jupiter – Animals, business ventures, celebration, force expansion and wealth magick.

FRIDAY – Venus – Arts, beauty, fertility,

glamour, growth, love magick and the earth element.

SATURDAY – Saturn – Banishing, binding, curses, hidden influences, initiation and secrets.

COLOR SYMBOLISM

Colors play a significant role in the perceptions of the mind. Looking at any color (specifically large blocked spaces like walls or colored-paper) you will see that colors make you "feel" a certain way. Play with each color in the spectrum by making cards to correspond. Using your intuition, "feel" the cards with your eyes open. And then again with your eyes closed. The next step is to attempt to "feel" and dist-inguish the colors on the cards without looking.

Candles, altar dressings, robes, talismanic squares and amulet stones are all use in magickal workings based on their color assoc-iations. For example: red candles draw love and black altar dressings banish evil.

WHITE – purity, truth, healing, full moon, Monday.

RED – passion, sex, love, strength, courage,

Tuesday.

ORANGE – power, healing, success, attraction, Sunday.

YELLOW – communication, mind, confidence, Sunday.

GREEN – fertility, renewal, Earth, fortune, Friday.

BLUE – tranquility, peace, understanding, Thursday.

PURPLE – wisdom, psychic, spirits, Wednesday.

BROWN – money, business, animals, the home.

GRAY – cancellation, stalemate, neutrality.

BLACK – banishing, hexing, loss, evil, Saturday.

KEYS OF MAGICK

The first ingredient is *desire*. It is imperative that the sorcerer truly desires the result of the magick with total self in order for the change to occur more rapidly this way. The purpose of magick is to ensure the outcome of what one *desires*. You must *desire* something hard enough to move the energy. [Ritual operations can compliment this.]

Desire alone does not create change – the *timing* is also important. The target of the energy being moved should be most receptive to the magick to be affected. Personal targets can be most easily influenced in their sleep (or at night) when the subconscious is most active. Any "planner" can tell you that improper *timing* in the implementation of a goal can be more counterproductive then "waiting to strike."

Visualization and *imagery* allow one to peak their imagination process. Focusing energy on a representing image allows the proper direction of that energy than simply calling out a name or such. In magickal workings, like forces attract like forces – the reason for the specific color and forms.

The energy raised through ritual must have a specific *direction*. Anxiety and other un-clarity will detract from the desired results. It is quite common for novices to worry about their workings. Understand however that dwelling on the energy spent can keep that energy fixed on you when it should be released (directed) into the universe. Rather than a physical action being taken with unseen results – sorcerer's direct energy in an unseen way that produces physical results. These results can take some time to manifest in the condensed physically perceived world.

CORRESPONDENCES

Magickal Correspondences are based on the occult concept that "like attracts like" forces. The lists which follow are similar to those found in many New Age "how-to" books. They are symbolic representations to enhance the sorcerer's personal vibrations during ritual.

Are these required to be followed for effective magick? No – but they are decent "fine-tuning" devices when using "ritual magick" systems. The basic lists given are "universal" in that they comply with most accepted source texts – but personalization is also a requirement of magick, so they can be amended so long as the sorcerer has purposeful intent in doing so.

THE ELEMENT OF AIR

Direction – east
Rules – intellect, mental, thought, knowledge,
    wind, mountain-tops, fields, clouds,
    vapor, storms, purification, new

beginnings.
Time – dawn
Season – spring
Color – yellow (purple)
Zodiac – gemini, libra, aquarius
Tools – wand, incense, visualization
Fragrances – frankincense, lavender,
    rosemary
Faeries – sylphs, pixies
Animals – all birds
King – Paralda

THE ELEMENT OF FIRE

Direction – south
Rules – creativity, change, transformation,
    flame, destruction, volcanoes, sexuality,
    passion, energy.
Time – noon
Season – summer
Color – red (green)
Zodiac – sagittarius, aries, leo
Tools – dagger, sword, staff, candles
Fragrances – orange, lime, citron
Faeries – salamanders, firedrakes, phoenix
Animals – snakes, reptiles
King – Djin

THE ELEMENT OF WATER

Direction – west
Rules – emotional, feeling, intuition, love,
    fertility, oceans, rains, wells, cleansing,
    dreams, subconscious, sleep, psychic.
Time – dusk
Season – autumn
Color – blue (orange)
Zodiac – cancer, scorpio, pisces
Tools – chalice, cauldron, mirror
Fragrances – camphor, lemon, lily-of-the-
    valley
Faeries – undines, merfolk, sirens, naiads
Animals – all fish and marine life
King – Niksa

THE ELEMENT OF EARTH

Direction – north
Rules – physical body, nature, foundations,
    solidity, success, money, death, forests,
    trees, animals, crystals.
Time – midnight
Season – winter
Color – green / black (white)
Zodiac – capricorn, taurus, virgo
Tools – pentacle, stones, salt, herbs

Fragrances – sage, pine, ceder, cypress
Faeries – elves, gnomes, dwarves
Animals – all four-footed
King – Ghob

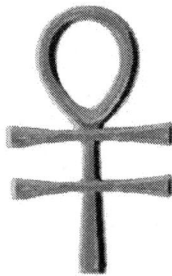

BASIC TECHNIQUES

THE MAGICK CIRCLE

All ritual magick is performed within the confines of a magick circle. These areas of working are made in different ways depending on the tradition – some in circles of trees (called "groves) or in circles of stones (called "henges"). Some magickal grimoires suggest the use of flour or chalk to mark the physical boundary of a circle on the ground. Others draw two or even three circles!

The purpose of the magick circle (literally "mandala") is to keep the energies raised within the circle, "in", and to protect against the energies of the outside world. The circle, when used for a magickal working, is called a "nemeton" (meaning "sacred space"). This area should only be used for magickal workings and mystical studies.

The location of the nemeton is up to you. Some wizards in the medieval times devoted entire rooms, towers or dungeons for these purposes – other more natural or shamanic practitioners use the outdoors as a means to get in touch with the powers of "Nature".

The size of the circle itself depends on the number of participants using the nemeton, and is also dependent on the sufficient space able to be dedicated to these purposes. Solitary practitioners often use their own height as the diameter.

Circles are a powerful geometric symbol, one of the most basic shapes next to the square, triangle and cross-pattern, which is most often equated with perfection, unity and recursive-infinity. The circle is feminine in vibration, typically representative of the water element. The term is, however, somewhat ambiguous in New Age terminology, referring sometimes to the group or coven and sometimes to the sacred area of working (*nemeton*) itself. The circle is the most sacred and prominent symbol found in all of sacred geometry.

The Sumerians discovered that a circle had 360 degrees. The concept first accepted as "religious belief" before it was proven with mathematics. Later, the Egyptians immediately began making calculations for Pi, starting with 256/81 or 256 divided by 81. This calculates as

3.16(04938…), which is somewhat close to the 3.14 approximation first used by the Greek Archimedes (c. 250 BC). [Actually, Archimedes used 223/71 and 22/7 to describe Pi.]

CASTING A CIRCLE

In every system, tradition and grimoire, from the highest form of ceremonial magick to the most primitive exercises of shamanism, magick is operated from within a sacred space, often called a nemeton (from Elvish-Druid vocabulary). In nearly every instance, a circle represents the nemeton. Permanent circles of stones, called henges, appear throughout Europe (e.g. *Stonehenge*) and among the Native Americans in the form of the Medicine Wheel. The wizard acknowledges that the space of the ritual circle exists apart from "ordinary" reality.

On the one hand, the circle represents a *microcosm* of the Greater Universe. The four directions define the "ends" of the Universe, often called watchtowers. Candles, elemental tablets or stations ritually recognize these elemental wards or thresholds. The tools or elemental weapons represent movements of energy, corresponding to the appropriate vibration. The wizard manipulates these objects with ritualistic intention and symbolically represents the desired changes and manifestation in the Universe. The ritual circle is also a *macrocosm* of the "inner world," "metaphysical world" and "subatomic world" represented outwardly with concrete symbols of abstractions and the indescribable nature of emotions and thoughts. These are represented via ritual drama and managed like a creative psychologist.

The circle is embodied by a physical boundary (many grimoires suggest chalk, flour or salt) though visualization is more powerfully employed. Examples of this are found in the Rituals of the Pentagram, particularly the *Lesser Banishing Ritual* of the Pentagram LBRP.

The *Watchtower Ceremony* is an even more advanced method of casting a circle in ceremonial magick. All of these examples require using a staff or sword to trace the circle physically on the ground, followed by defining the boundary of the nemeton in the air (at about waist height) using a wand or other magickal weapon (of simply your hand).

While tracing, the operator projects a blue ray of light to form a protective band. Remember, the key to a successful circle casting is to recognize a separation between ordinary space and sacred space. The magick circle represents the chessboard of the wizard's reality. The "pieces" are put in place during a manageable predetermined ritual setting. Just before the end of the working, this personal reality is projected (uploaded) into the Universal Consciousness. In other words, by performing ritual magick, you are affecting the Universe by intentionally projecting the personal energies that you have stored up, perfected and refined within the nemeton. People actually affect reality everyday with their actions, emotions and thoughts. By intentionally doing so with more disciplined faculties and focus, the wizard is able to use these natural laws at will.

The most basic methods of circle-casting require only visualization and energy. Go to the eastern quarter of your circle and use your index (power) finger on your projective hand (the one you write with or right hand) and draw the boundary of the circle as you walk clockwise or sun-wise (to the south, etc.) and return again to the east. This completes the boundary of the circle. The key is to charge your projective arm with personal energy and release it through your finger as you mark the boundary. This energy should be visualized as "blue" and the circle becomes known as the "circle of protections" or COPs.

Some people will also have "elemental" candles or lamps burning at each direction – yellow in the east, red in the south, blue in the west and green in the north. Not only do these aid the sorcerer in being more aware of the energies of each direction, but they can assist later when you call upon these elemental energies. Most ritual and ceremonial magick in this dimension is oriented to the four-fold elements that constitute the "Gates" or "Watchtowers" of the Universe.

The following ritual text is derived from the Book of Shadows (BOS) of the Elven Fellowship Circle of Magick (EFCOM). This rite calls on "Awen" and "Menw," incorporates elements of the "Watchtower Ceremony," and the Elven Guardians of the elemental weapons derived from the Tuatha d'Anu lore of the Celtic/Druid traditions. The text was originally written for groups (coven or grove), but can be adapted by solitary practitioners. It can be supplemented with any ceremonial rite (e.g. calling elementals).

CASTING A CIRCLE

A. East: "We consecrate this circle of power to Menw and Awen."

B. South: "May they hear our calls and bless us with power."

C. West: "May the Elder Gods, the Shinning Ones, aid and protect us."

D. North: "We stand at a threshold between worlds in a veil of mystery."

E. East: "Oh-roh Ee-bah Ah-oh-zod-pee. In the names and letters of the Great Eastern Quadrangle, I invoke thee spirits of the Watchtower of the East."

F. South: "Oh-ee-peh Teh-ah-ah Peh-doh-keh. In the names and letters of the Great Southern Quadrangle, I invoke thee spirits of the Watchtower of the South."

G. West: "Em-peh-heh Ar-ess-el Gah-ee-oh-leh. In the names and letters of the Great Western Quadrangle, I invoke thee spirits of the Watchtower of the West."

H. North: "Moh-ar Dee-ah-leh Heh-keh-teh-gah. In the names and letters of the Great Northern Quadrangle, I invoke thee spirits of the Watchtower of the North."

I. East: "May the forces of the Watchtowers be present among us."

J. South: "Let us now conjure the powers of the

Masters."

K. West: "And may with their powers come the wisdom to use it."

L. North: "From the northern city of Falias, I summon Master Morfessa. Bring the Stone of Fal and stand as Guardian of the North."

M. East: "From the eastern city of Gorias, I summon Master Esras. Bring the mighty Spear of Lugh and stand as Guardian of the East."

N. South: "From the southern city of Finias, I summon Master Uscias. Bring the Sword of Nuada and stand as Guardian of the South."

O. West: "From the western city of Murias, I summon Master Semias. Bring the Cauldron of the Dagda and stand as Guardian of the West."

P. North: "May the energies of the Four Masters gather among us here."

CALLING THE ELEMENTALS

After the circle has been cast, the sorcerer can call on the elemental beings that dwell on the astral plane. Some sorcerers incorporate this step into their circle casting. The elemental beings can aid you in magickal workings as powerful co-magicians – and they should be treated with respect.

Go to the east and proclaim:

Ye spirits of Air, Elemental Sylphs of the East. I call thee here now to aid in the magick I shall perform. So mote it be.

Go to the south and proclaim:

Ye spirits of the Fire, Elemental Salamanders of the South. I call thee here now to aid in the magick I shall perform. So mote it be.

Go to the west and proclaim:

Ye spirits of the Water, Elemental Undines of the West. I call thee here now to aid in the magick I shall perform. So mote it be.

Go to the north and proclaim:

Ye spirits of the Earth, Elemental Gnomes of the North. I call thee here now to aid in the magick I shall perform. So mote it be.

Using the magickal key of "visualization" you

can see an elemental being of proper elemental traits coming to the edge of your circle from the given direction. It should be made clear that they are there, but the sorcerer may need to initiate the exchange of energy with willpower and visualization.

CALLING DEITIES

After the elementals (or lesser beings) the sorcerer can call on any personal deities or archetypes that might aid in the magickal working. Some of the more religious systems of magick have adopted sacred pantheons from the Celts, Norse, Egyptians, Romans, Babylonians, Sumerians, Greeks and the like.

Virtually every culture has a similar mythos that can be utilized in magick – and each is part of an authentic religious tradition.

A modern example, Wicca, evokes the powers of duality through the "god" and "goddess", and following with the ancient example, will often have representations of each present on the altar.

A Call to the Goddess:

Goddess of the Starry Skies, Goddess of the Fertile Plain, Goddess of the Oceans' Sighs, Goddess of the Gentle Rain. Hear my calling to you this hour. Open wide the Gate of Mystic Light. Waken me with your graceful power. Aid me in my magickal rite.

A Call to the God:

Great God of the Forest Deep, Master of the animals and Sun. Here in a world lost to sleep, now that the day is done [just begun]. I call to you in the ancient way, here in this circle round. I desire my will to be displayed and I call you to send your powers down.

CLOSING THE CIRCLE

As a sorcerer it is essential that you show respect for the energies and entities with are called to aid your workings. It is customary to work "backwards" beginning with the dismissal of the "god" and "goddess" (deities) followed by the elementals. For the elementals go to the north and dismiss them in each direction working counter-clockwise. Ask each to return promptly to their place of dwelling but to come again to your aid when called.

51

The last necessary part of ritual magick is extinguishing and grounding the energies of the circle that you cast. You can do multiple things to accomplish this. Some will go to the north and travel the boundary of the circle counter-clockwise using the receptive hand, retracing the lines.

An alternative to this could be to ground the circle by standing in the centre of the circle with arms upraised. Visualize the circle of energy being sent down, deep into the ground... deep...deeper – down into the fiery centre of the Earth. This is often literally called "grounding" (and I have recently seen "earthing" as well).

RAISING ENERGY

In all magickal operations, the wizard is respon-sible for handling (channeling) the mystical energy that enables thoughts to manifest in the Universe. There are two basic types (sources) of energy encountered: a) personal or internal power and b) external forces. Ritualism, spell-craft and ceremonial magick all depend on the balanced blend of these two energetic forms.

Using only your own stores of personal energy

will leave you feeling drained, possibly depressed and more susceptible to magickal warfare (via a weakened aura). On the contrary, channeling only the overtly powerful external energies without tempering/filtering with you own personal energetic system will result negatively or as wild magick. The best way to understand this is to compare the idea to electricity.

The external power that is transmitted to your house is unusable without first "stepping it down" with a "transformer," which offers the same "energy potential," but alters the voltage to something useable at your outlets (e.g. 400,000 volts to 120 volts). Using personal power alone would be the same as draining a battery or auxiliary generator without supplementing it with external power sources.

The ability to raise energy is paramount to the success of your magick. In personal developmental systems and apprenticeships, the skills of energy use are among the first practical lessons to be encountered. The process of raising energy draws on the most fundamental skills (breathing techniques, grounding, visualization, thought discipline and willpower) and puts them into constructive personal use.

The seeker will find applications of energy used in casting a circle or raising a cone of power during the initial phases of ritual working. The nemeton is conjured with personal energy and becomes your metaphysical catalyst or "transformer" for the external energy that is called in (e.g. calling elementals, drawing down the Moon (or Sun), dragon calling, Enochian Magick, Goetic evocation, etc.). Using pore-breathing techniques, you can actually absorb an external energetic current or ray of light and internalize it.

Neo-paganism, the Wicca tradition and even neodruidism seek to revive old archaic pantheons of the "old religions" so that these traditions can be remembered. Most revivals of specific regional-cultural systems work from a "table of deities" comparable to the powers of the saints that are called upon by Catholics and Santerians.

Whether integrated into spellcraft or a more formal seasonal celebration, those practicing a system that is aligned to a particular culture will call on the names and powers of appropriate "archetypes" from that pantheon. For example, when raising energy for love magick, the operator may also call forth energy from the deity of love that corresponds to the pantheon they are working form (Aphrodite-Greek, Isis-Egyptian, etc.). The diversity found in the New Age has even led to the formation of eclectic systems that blend pantheons and call on all multi-cultural representations of an aspect. This is okay as long as the practitioner is fully aware of the symbolism and tradition behind all of the deities and pantheons to be incorporated.

Raising energy can be a challenging part of the magickal process. Not only is it crucial to the success of the ritual working, it is also the most "misrepresented" and "misrelayed" topic learned from New Age books. Chanting, singing, drumming and dancing (music in general) are commonly used in shamanic and indigenous Nature-oriented systems as a means of drawing a swelling power with the *nemeton*. Muscle tensing, absorbing and storing a cumulative draw of energy in the physical body, is just as common.

Variations on the muscle technique can include visualization of an orb or ball of energy that your form between your hands. Personal energy and external energy is pushed in to the "energy ball" and then directed (released) via intention. The *Middle Pillar Rite* from the Golden Dawn

System helps to raise energy for high magick by activating the chakras (personal energetic system).

Before raising energy, perform any preliminary grounding and relaxation methods that are necessary to bring your mind to magickal state. Then conjure your nemeton. Seated within, begin rubbing your palms together, back and forth. Begin slowly at first, then progressively increase the rate. As you do this, you may notice that the muscles in your body naturally becoming tense. Continue to do this as you feel the energy swell and begin to accumulate. When you feel the energy peak, before you are going to slow down, stop and pull you hands a few inches apart. Focus your attention between them and then slowly move your hands apart and then close together, repeatedly in sweeping motions. See and feel the energetic orb or sphere manifesting before you. Charge it with your intentions (via visualization) and focus any external bands of energy into it, then release it to the Universe, carrying the intention of your goal to the Akashic Records and back again (to manifest). Take note of the personal energy used during the process. You may feel fatigued afterward, so eat light and rest.

AUTOSUGGESTION

The magick of the subconscious mind – the part of the human brain that dictates reality for you. It is within the power of the subconscious mind to utterly change the perception of reality. This has an affect on the global or universal consciousness, which is like a shared reality. This is what causes others to be influenced by your reality, especially those who are openly allowing the change.

The subconscious is thought to be most receptive during sleep. Likewise, when dealing with magick on others, performing the workings while they are sleeping can allow the energy to affect their subconscious will. Using the subconscious allows one to believe something to the degree of making it real – manifesting it into existence. Humans believe they are dependent on certain habits and systems, but by going in an programming the subconscious, reality becomes changed and the true magick happens!

THREE CATEGORIES OF SORCERER

SEX – Sorcerers who are sexually appealing

and exceptionally charismatic – they are enticing and beautiful. They use their looks and sex appeal as a powerful weapon towards others.

SENTIMENT – Sorcerers who are eccentric and live the "village witch" lifestyle where they're enchantments offer wonder to children and adults alike. They are the stereotyped versions of the witches, warlocks and magicians. They have their herbs, candles and incense well-displayed, and trinkets everywhere to capture the eye.

WONDER – Sorcerers who take time to alter their physical appearance for the outer purposes – goths and teenaged vampyres especially apply. Those who wear the black dressings, heavy make-up, altered hair-styles and blatantly "walk-the-walk". These are figures that most contemporary society stays away from for fear of simply "pissing them off".

WICCA AND THE
WITCHCRAFT REVIVAL

It was not until 1951 that the Anti-Witchcraft & Magick Acts were appealed and the public practice of magick was no longer punishable by imprisonment or death. Magickal organizations and secret societies had previously existed seeking to perfect ceremonial magick (such as the Hermetic Order of the Golden Dawn) and figures like Aleister Crowley has already been consider-ed "witches." An intensive revival interest in the witchcraft tradition was occurring in the late 19th Century independent of the ceremonial elitists, claiming a more rural peasant-orientation to mysticism, including a return to such paradigms as the gypsy folk traditions and "old wives' tales."

Three influential literary works appeared in 1890, which set the stage for the wiccan, neodruidic and neo-pagan movements of the 20th Century. *The Golden Bough*, written by Sir. James Frazer, is a monumental treatise classifying diverse folk and pagan traditions and customs, particularly those concerning Nature. The work became very influential among neodruids, not so much from the opinions and interpretations, but because of the vast amount of folklore condensed within. Mac-Gregor Mathers translated the notorious grimoire, the *Keys of Solomon*. Most of the initial interest was limited to fellow members of the Golden Dawn (GD), but it later became a strong influence on Wicca. Finally, Charles Leland, a historian of the gypsy and Strega traditions, published *Aradia: Gospel of the Witches*, presented as a secret oral tradition that led underground witches since the 14th Century.

In 1921, an anthropologist and Egyptologist named Margaret Murray, author of *The Witch-cult in Western Europe*, reinvestigated the works mentioned above. This is what sparked Gerald Gardner's revival of witchcraft in the form of "Wicca," drawn from an old Anglo-Saxon root meaning "wise" or "wild." The tradition, and the Book of Shadows used to found it, received input by two other figures seldom credited with any part of the founding of Wicca: Aleister Crowley and Ross Nichols. The tradition borrows the ritual magick of ceremonialism, the correspondences of occult philosophy (*The Keys of Solomon* and *The Magus*). It draws from native Gypsy and Strega traditions of Eastern Europe and its *Old Ways*, coupled with Celtic, Druidic and Norse myst-icism from Western Europe.

Neodruidism and most magickal organizations and secret societies were predominantly solar (Sun) orient-ed, whereas Wicca aligned its system to the Moon with an emphasis on the "goddess," a focus that is not found extensively in Medieval and Renaissance magickal styles. Gardner's tradition (also called "Gardnerian Wicca") also promoted skyclad work within covens.

In the 1960s, Alexander Sanders ("Alexandrian Wicca") became a self-proclaimed "King of the Witches," leading an alternate wiccan tradition that placed a heavier emphasis on ceremonial magick and grimoire use.

Many of the facets of the overall system are quite old, but those who subscribe to the New Age eclectic tradition of the wiccan outline are practicing a system that was consolidated less then 100 years ago. It has also given rise to 1,000 derived traditions that are obviously younger. The lure of the magickal tradition, the ability to possess books of magick and don the wizard's cap has captivated curious minds for centuries and true seekers have found this lifestyle by one means or another. The great archetype of magick is universal, but also open to interpretation by a cultural consciousness and the individual psyche. The overwhelming inclination to pass manuscripts or ritual texts off as "older" than they are is an abundant concern in all forms of mysticism. It is, however, counterproductive to personal magickal development to get caught up in the whirlwind of origin and authenticity debates. Oral traditions and even personal (or family) systems have always operated in a mysterious manner and become even more cryptic when first transcribed into the written word.

Witchcraft has been misinterpreted, according to the New Age, as merely a feminine alternative to "masculine wizardry." In Wicca, gender dualism is recognized. It would have to be, especially given that all of the prominent figures throughout the decades (Gerald Gardner, Isaac Bonewits, Alex Sanders, Raymond Buckland, Scott Cunningham, etc.) have been male! The covens, however, appear to be led by a High Priestess, who is considered spiritually superior to any priest. Some Dianic forms of Wicca are open to females only. A significant increase of interest in Wicca emerged in the mid-1990s as a result of the motion picture, *The*

Craft, which exclusively depicted young girls practicing magick. What is peculiar about this fad-appeal to Wicca is that the movie did not really depict Wicca at all so much as a Hollywood presentation of ceremonial and ritualized high magick. The "fictitious" grimoire used in the movie, *The Invocation of the Spirit*, was actually a copy of Waite's *Book of Ceremonial Magick* (although the lightning-storm drawing does not appear in it, nor do any of the rituals the girls practiced).

In the 21st Century, "Wicca" has become a household catchall term for many aspects of the New Age. What is actually practiced today is minimally based on the work of "Gardnerian" or "Alexandrian" interpretations. Some aspects of neodruidism overlap into the varying wiccan traditions and elements from all systems of magick, whether primitive shamanism or the *Sacred Book of Magick of Abramelin the Mage*, seem to be fair game. While some practitioners fault others for not knowing "their" version of the mystic practices, too many variations exist to qualify one or another as a "purer" strain.

COVENS, CIRCLES & GROUPS

A social unit from which the Wicca and witchcraft traditions operate. The earliest reference to the term "coven" dates back to 14th Century Ireland. The semantics appear nearly synonymous with similar rooted words, "convene" and "covenant." The New Age has seen an arrival of larger "schools" and "churches" of these traditions, but the majority of practitioners rely on a smaller coven unit as a basis for operations. Each coven operates completely independent from others, overseeing the adherence to the main principles of belief without have to report to a hierarchical authority outside of the coven.

A strict traditionalist might tell you that a true coven must have exactly thirteen members, the number of annual lunar cycles. Depending on the flavor of leader-ship, there may be twelve members and a High Priestess or a High Priest (King of the Witches), or even eleven members and a leader of each sex. This is typical of "closed covens" or "family traditions" that do not openly invite membership. At reaching thirteen members, a coven may opt to "close" their membership, or if necessary, have members leave to form shoot-off covens that best meet individual needs. Group magick is delicate and requires the right number of participants. Too few will not move enough energy and with too many it is often hard to focus energy properly on a single goal. By modern definitions, a coven is simply a group, whether study oriented or experimental.

"Training covens" will typically have two different "circles" or subgroups. The Outer Court or Outer Circle serves to initiate and apprentice novices that have less than two years experience with the coven. The Inner Circle is responsible for dispensing the teachings maintained by the coven and leading ritual operations. The Outer Court participates with the Inner Circle in all sabbat and esbat cyclic observations. The Inner Court will also come together to "coven" independently of the Outer Circle, discussing the rites and formulas of their tradition and experimenting in advanced practices that the members of the Outer Circle have yet to be introduced to. Depending on the size and needs of a coven, a wyvern coven may also be established for the young.

Contrary to what many traditionalists may tell you, the coven is not a necessary part of the magickal life. There are actually far more solitary practitioners out there buying books, taking classes and inheriting traditions from past generations, than actually practice magick in conventional covens. The craft term has also expanded to include other magickal paths not specific to the "religion" of Wicca. In fact, many general magick covens consist of agnostics, Gnostics, neodruids, Norse-revivalists and Unitarian-Universalists (among others).

The knowledge of the New Age has also expanded over the years, revealing that the heart of every indigenous culture contains some magickal tradition and interpretation of the deities, the Sky Gods, who "from the heavens, to Earth came" and the avatar-like heroes they bred. A coven will typically align themselves to a specific cultural mythos and pantheon (though many eclectic covens also exist).

It is not recommended that novices start their own "covens." An individual can be powerful, even more powerful than an entire coven, but groups can move large amounts of energy quickly when properly directed. Having several inexperienced practitioners dabbling together unchecked is simply the prelude for a catastrophe. The suggestion of the current author is for interested individuals to first form "study groups" to pursue the material academically before becoming concerned with flashy "ranks" and "titles" and all of the other drama that can be associated with group magick. Members of the "study group" can come together to learn and discuss, experiment individually and then reconvene to compare notes.

The purpose of a coven shouldn't be mis-construed as simply a vehicle for group magick. Covens may not even perform traditional "magick," coming together only to ritually ob-serve seasonal and astronomical celebrations. These operations seldom connect with the type of archaic currents of energy that can get you into trouble. Group participation in spellcraft, on the other hand, can be challenging. All of the participants have to be raising energy and visualizing in synch with each other. Therefore, the obvious recommendation is to perfect your magickal skills as a solitary practitioner before merging those energies with the "group consciousness." The goal of the group ritual must be reasonable to all involved. Those in disagreement or even disinterest should not participate. Some traditions observe methods like the cone of power to help maintain the harmony of raised energy.

GROVE FESTIVALS

There are eight "grove festivals" which have been recalled from the lore and mysteries of the ancient wizards and mystics. They mark specific times of year that have both astronomical and agricultural significance on the planet for those who work and live in harmony with the earth ways. The current model of the "wheel of the year" is common in contemporary neo-paganism.

The traditionally observed "new year" festival in the New Age is called *Samhain* (pronounced "sow-en") and it is the original celebration of Halloween. The eve of October 31st into the month of November. It is a time in honor of the "dead names" - our ancestors, dress up in your finest costumary and perform dark rites in the secrecy of the forest around a "bone"-fire.

Yule is the original pagan celebration of Christmas, a time in hon-or of the oncoming rebirth of the Sun "god" child at the winter solstice (usually December 21-22). The Yule Log, Christmas Tree, use of mistletoe, holly and ivy are all customs from the ancient Druids and have now been integrated into contemporary living.

Imbolc is on February 1st and is now observed in this country as Groundhog's Day. It is an ancient candle festival also known in Western Europe as "Brighid's Day." It is a time of looking forward to the coming spring and customs include the creation and dressing of corn dolls to ensure a prosperous spring season.

The Spring Equinox is an ancient observation that is now common to Easter or *Ostara*. As with the Autumn Equinox the time and energies of day and night are balanced (usually March 21-22) and the Sun enters Aries. The hunt for eggs, pastel colors and the wearing of green clothing has all been handed down to us from the Celts.

May 1st marks the major fire festival now called "May Day", but the ancients knew it as *Beltaine*, literally the "fires of Bel" - a primordial name for "Lord of the Earth." Bonfires are lit and the maypole, representing the world tree and link between the upper and lower realms (in addition to the commonly thought fertility symbolism), was erected and danced around. This is the observation of the spring season turning to summer.

The Summer Solstice, as many are aware, is the

longest day of the year – the height of solar power annually. Visions of white-robed Druids ascending hills to stone circles to greet the morning sun on this day (usually June 21-22) are not uncommon.

Lughnassadh marks the beginning of the harvest season with the "wedding festival" of the Celtic stellar-deity, Lugh. The height of the harvest is marked with the Autumn Equinox, equivalent to our modern "sentiments" behind Thanksgiving Day (minus the aboriginal genocide). This was a time for the rural-pagan agricultural folk to give thanks to the "spirits of the harvest" and the "spirits of the wine" and the "spirits of the grain" and so forth. Thus is the "wheel of the year" - bringing us full circle back to *Samhain*.

MAGICKAL NAMES

When you begin to use magick, being to address spirits or when you are initiated into a magickal circle, you will assume an identity that is separate from the world or society of everyday men. To make this even more apparent it is not uncommon for sorcerers to take on new "magick" names, sometimes called "circle names" or "secret names."

My magickal name is "Merlyn Stone" and I don't exactly keep that a secret – but people do not always know me by both my magickal name and my birth name – which can certainly provide me with the anonymity necessary to gain employment and interact with the outside world. The names are seldom used together – you aren't supposed to hail down your pagan friend "Jeff" in the grocery story by calling out his coven name "Eternal Flame." etc.

RITUAL DRESS

Since the sorcerer assumes a different identity than is assumed in the norm, the street clothes don't quite fit in either. But sometimes this cannot be helped.

There are times when one just feels like getting decked out in make-up, eye-shadow, chokers, cuffs, black with crystals, talismans and penta-grams dangling from every possible recess. This isn't always and it isn't for every-one, but when you are in the privacy of your "coven" or even your own bedroom, you have a chance to explore the shadow part of yourself that seeks the embrace.

Some wiccans follow a bit of a departure from the norm on this and work *skyclad*, which is "dressed by the sky" or nude. Given that Gerald Gardner was a nudist, this comes as no surprise, but it certainly is not required – nor is it necessarily a gateway to ritual abuse. I personally have a hard time with this one.

PRINCIPLES OF BELIEF

One upon a time (in 1974) there was a grand convocation of witches in my home town of Minneapolis. There, the wiccan elders formed a council to unify wicca under a certain codex or doctrine of beliefs that could be met on a universal basis. They numbered them, much like a series of by-laws, and wrote them in a straight-forward fashion so as not to have future generations misinterpret them.

They are (in edited form):

1. Rituals are to be performed in accordance with Nature, the seasons and phases of the moon.
2. We seek harmony with Nature and believe in ecological responsibility.
3. All have the potential of magick, even if it

is not outright apparent.

4. We believe that the creative force is dual, equal in both male and female aspects.

5. We acknowledge the outer world of the physical as well as the psychological realm of the mind.

6. We honor those who have wisdom to offer, but do not recognize an authoritarian system.

7. Religion, wisdom, witchcraft and magick are combined to form the wiccan way.

8. One is not a witch unless they live in harmony with Nature. The title alone is meaningless.

9. We believe in the continuation of life, the evolution and development of consciousness.

10. We do not deny others the freedom to believe in their ways. They should respect ours.

11. The debate of the history of witchcraft and the terminology therein is not our concern.

12. We do not acknowledge the existence of an absolute evil or devil figure and therefore don't worship one.

13. We believe we should seek Nature for health, well-being and holistic medicines.

THE ARTS OF SPELLCRAFT

SPELLCRAFT SIMPLIFIED

Did you know that just tying your shoes was an act of spellcraft or magick? Don't argue with me, yet! The act of spellcraft is to cause a change in accordance with your will, or to make something happen because you want it to. Thus, no matter the means, tying your shoes because you want them tied and causing this manip-ulated change in physical reality is spellcraft! Of course, you don't think about it like this, but essentially that is what it is. If you look at spellcraft in this way, you will find it very simple to master. But how does a spell work?

The circle is cast, energy is raised, the goal is visualized and energy is released to that outcome. The circle is finally extinguished. Herbs, incense, candles, incantations, etc. are aids in attracting the proper energy. In all forms of magick, especially spellcraft, like attracts like forces or energies. If you want to attract the energy of love and send raised energy of that nature to the outcome, then you need to surr-ound yourself with the tools and aids that will help you in attaining a specific energetic current. Spellcraft is limited only by the sorcerer's imagination. You can also use the correspondences found throughout this book to further supplement this ideal.

SPELLCRAFT UNVEILED

Also called "low magick," this practice is the most common method of ritualized use of intention and willpower taught in the New Age. The purpose of the art is to direct the energy of the desires and will of the operator through dramatic representations. [Anthropologists recognize this practice among indigenous shamans in the form of sympathetic magick.]

Spellcraft is most often concerned with influencing change in the mundane/physical world such as fertility, wealth and love. The main tenet is that the currents of energy attached to you in the future are based on the raised energy of emotions, thoughts and actions of the present. Jesus said: "Ask and it shall be given; knock and the door will open." The wizard learns the more successful questions to "ask" and best means of "knocking."

Conventional spellcraft and prayer are essentially the same. Most religious practitioners are not instructed in the proper and most effective ways to pray, leaving them at the mercy of established organizations for any real "divine intervention." But the wizard does not wait for "divine intervention." The New Age teaches that you are the only one responsible for your own life. God has given you the mental and spiritual faculties to recognize the Right Way to Ascension. Through proper focus, emotional purity and intention of will, you can attract any ray of light into your life.

The definition of spellcraft is really "to see any transformational manifestation occur in the physical world in accordance with will." It doesn't matter what means are used, setting and meeting goals for change is a unique awareness of the human mind: you can affect the future by acting in the present. This is no small realization since it has allowed humans to rise above the Animal Kingdom and establish "human civilization." The truth is: if your intention is to see something through, it doesn't really matter if you accomplish this by some form of telepathy or simply some old fashioned hard work (according to Freemasonry).

Hopefully, you are traveling a path of the lease resistance so as to use the most appropriate energy type in the best way to accomplish your goals.

Ritualized spellcraft can be operated closely to the practices of ceremonial magick, though they tend to have more mundane ends in mind. The use of elemental tablets, elemental weapons, herbs, incense, robes and cloaks can supplement the basic formula of spellcraft. Candle magick is especially useful. Your working can be as simple or elaborate as you deem necessary. The additional tools and implements can be included only if they actually help you to connect with the desired currents of energy. They should be removed as distractions if they do not assist. For this reason a controlled environment, whether hidden away in Nature or in a room dedicated to magick, should be used. [There should be no non-magickal distractions in the nemeton area.] In traditions of high magick, the ritual chambers are often designed with specific parameters in mind and even the lodges of secret societies are reserved for ceremonial purposes only.

Almost every author in the New Age teaches the arts of spellcraft differently. Most texts include the preliminary steps that a sorcerer should have developed prior to these attempts. The abilities to be grounded, focused, use breathing techniques and enter the body of light are all paramount to ritual success prior to the "casting of the spell." Graphic representations of your intentions (pictures, symbols, glyphs) should be prepared ahead of time and the operator must be very familiar with the intended working prior to the physical enactment. [Not doing so accounts for many of the initial failures for practitioners using spellcraft.]

It is possible to be too concerned with the "ritual text" itself during practice, which will not keep the energy of your work where you want it. The present sorcerer can easily make use of this process by referencing the links found in the steps below.

The Sevenfold Spellcraft Formula

1. Casting a Circle (conjuring the nemeton)
2. Calling Elementals (conjuring external powers)
3. Raising Energy (personal blended with conjured)
4. Visualization (seeing the change as

presently occurring)
5. Releasing Energy (see *raising
energy*)
6. Dismissal of Spirits (closing
formalities)
7. Extinguishing the Circle (banishing
residual energy)

The adepts of the ages always advise operators not to dwell on their workings once completed. It is a common mistake made among novices to worry about the effectiveness of the ritual. Once the energy raised in energy has been conscious-ly released into the Akasha of the Universe, allow it the chance to resonate and vibrate. If you recall this energy back from the Universe with your thoughts, it won't be "out there" working for you. One common suggestion is to sleep afterward and allow the subconscious process to equalize naturally. This is not usual-ly difficult since most spellcraft operations are performed at night under the correlative lunar and planetary influences.

TOOLS OF THE ART

Rituals magick incorporates specific symbolic implements into the rites that the sorcerer must either construct or find. Most of they are attributed to the elements. The sorcerer represents the "fifth element" in the ritual, both surrounded and embodied by the four. The Akashic Box or storage chest can also be thought of as a "fifth elemental" tool used to keep the tools safe from prying eyes.

The Wand – whenever one thinks of witches and wizards the "magick wand" immediately is conjured to mind. This is not purely a fanciful stereotype as the wand represents the "air element" in ritual. In folk traditions they are often made of wood. Hazel and Elder make good multipurpose wands. Other associations are apple and love, ash and healing, pine and prosperity, rowan and protection or birch and purification. Willow is also a common wand. They average about fifteen inches long and half an inch thick – placed in the east during rituals.

The Blade (Dagger or Sword) – the magickal blade represents the will, force and desire of the sorcerer. As if not already apparent, this tool represents the fire element. Herbalists will also have a separate knife used for the cutting of plants, herbs and roots.

The Cauldron – another common association

81

with the witches. Often used to have a controlled "fire-water" (burning alcohol) as well as the
"brewing" of potions and tinctures – essentially
a water tool, but very alchemical.

The Pentacle Stone – a circular plate of wood,
metal or stone (or even just a stone) – and I
have even seen a few wax ones – about six to
eight inches in diameter and half an inch thick.
Using sandpaper (if wood), the disk should be
finely sanded with the five-pointed star painted
or embedded into the plate with the tips reaching the ends of the disk (or a border line drawn
as a circle around the disk). The pentagram is a
sign of the race and also a symbol of elemental
balance (and protection) and represents the
earth element in rituals.

The Cup or Chalice – a true water elemental
tool used to hold water, wine and other liquids
(libations and ritual meads). The cup, chalice or
goblet can be fashioned from whatever materials seem fitting or available. Celtic lore speaks
of a "shell-chalice", for example.

Other tools to be kept on hand are a good
supply of incense, candles of various colors,
various herbs and types of gemstones.

MAGICK FOR OTHERS

Beginners may find this almost completely unsuccessful. Spellcraft requires intense emotions, needs and goals. The desire and willpower must be genuine to be powerful. This can be adventurous enough for one to access for their own benefit then alone the needs of another. If you do a "love spell" for yourself, then you fully understand the need and can feel the desire – this helps bring the manifestation. It may be very difficult to sufficiently raise the same level of energy for the gain of purely another.

Sorcery and magick is a powerful tool for one's own self-development and improvement and so it might actually be more beneficial to teach another the primary rules of spellcraft as opposed to actually doing the spell for them.

CANDLE MAGICK

Beeswax candles have been an integral part of mysticism and ceremonial magick for thousands of years. Their use in ritual is based on color, which correlates to the energy vibration they project. Prior to and during the operation they are "charged" with an intention or made to represent a particular person or object (target). While candles do appear in many operations, candle magick is also its own non-specific system that uses candles as a catalyst for directing energy, The symbolic representation of a candle is usually uttered out loud as it is lit to aid in focusing your attention.

Depending on your experience and visualization abilities, candle magick can be simply performed through meditation and prayer or as part of a more formalized method of spellcraft. As a means of sympathetic magick, candle magick requires imagination and creativity to be effective. Just as the wizard creates a microcosm of the Universe when creating a nemeton (or casting a circle) so too must candle magick be performed at an altar that represents the "chessboard of reality." By manipulating symbols on a representative playing field, you create a change first in your own consciousness, which is then projected into the reality at large. If you are drawing something to you, you need a candle to represent yourself and one for the energy you want to attract. For several successive nights (usually three or seven) you perform your working, each time moving the candle (that represents the external energy) closer to yours. The opposite can be done for operations of reversal or banishing. Operations of candle magick are most successful when the operator speaks an affirmation or intention vocally at each lighting and ritual action.

Along with the represented colored candles, there is also a candle that you will use to represent you. This can be placed in the center of the altar or working area, as the sorcerer works the "game of chess" from a cosmocentric perspective. If there is to be a candle representing another person, some spellcasters have found it helpful to use color specific candles based on the zodiac.

AQUARIUS – Blue	LEO – Red
PISCES – White	VIRGO – Gold/Black
ARIES – White	LIBRA – Black
TAURUS – Red	SCORPIO – Brown
GEMINI – Red	SAG. – Gold/Black
CANCER – Green	CAPRICORN – Red

CANDLE SPELLS

The following are simply examples of possible uses of candle magick. The sorcerer is encouraged to develop their own applications as needed.

AFFAIRS – to break up the love affair of another, use the two zodiacal colors of the people involved. Use also a black candle for the breakup, a brown for the dying love and a light green to cause jealousy and discord.

BAD HABITS – to overcome a bad habit, place a black candle in the middle representing the habit itself. Surround it with white candles (the defeating color of black) representing the defeat of the habit itself.

DREAMS – to cause prophetic dreams surround your candle with a blue candle of peace (a requirement dreaming). Use an orange candle to represent what you want to dream about and a white for sincerity and truth.

FEAR – to overcome the emotion of fear, surround your candle with several orange candles representing personal strength and self-confidence as well as the white candle of purity.

JEALOUSY – to arouse jealousy in another individual surround their candle with a few brown candles of hesitation and uncertainty. Use also light green to represent discord, illness and of course, jealousy.

MEDITATION – to aid in the act of prayer or meditation, surround your candle with light blue candles of peace and tranquility.

POWER – to gain powers over other people have both your candle and the candle of who you wish to control of the altar. Each day, move their candle closer to yours, which should be placed with a purple candle of power and an orange candle of attraction.

SPELLJAMMING – to remove a hex, curse or cross, surround your candle with red for strength and vigor. Use also white for purity and sincerity. Have a black and brown candle on either side. The black symbolizes the cursed spell and the brown represents the uncertainty of the castor. Move the black candle towards the brown (and away from yours) each day of the working. This will effectively deflect their spell.

HERBS

If used properly, herbs can be a potent ingredient for magickal spellcraft. Herbalism includes the use of dried herbs, incense, the construction of amulet bags and oil manufacture. Herbs can be added to the altar, burned in the candle's flame (or as an incense), worn as oils or perfume, and even placed in amulet bags to be carried.

The following are just a few examples of herbal energy associations:

> LUNAR – frankincense, sandalwood
> LOVE – rose, cinnamon, sandalwood, patchouli
> PEACE – bay/laurel, sandalwood
> WEALTH – cloves, nutmeg, poppy seed, cedar
> STUDYING – cinnamon, rosemary
> SUCCESS – benzoin, cinnamon, dragon's blood
> PROTECTION – frankincense, sandalwood, rosemary

Naturally, incense is burned during rituals and spells, but you may also burn it in your house after a working or spell to keep the energy active or resonant – be sure not to dwell on the working, however. You can also leave the house with a scented oil or amulet bag to carry the personal effects of a spell with you. The following are some of the more popular herbal applications:

ALL-SPICE – prosperity, relaxation
APPLE – love, happiness, relaxation
CAMPHOR – psychic power, letting go
CINNAMON – protection, sexual vigor
EUCALYPTUS – healing, purification
JASMINE – love, sleep, relaxation
MUSK – courage, sexual vigor
MYRRH – protection, purification, hex-breaking
PATCHOULI – peace of mind, sexual vigor
ROSE – love, peace, harmony, unity
SANDALWOOD – healing, protection

Satchets or "amulet bags" are four inch squares of cloth that you can place certain herbs (and other small items on) and tie up the corners to be carried pouch-like. It is important to recognize the color symbolism in both the fabric for the square and also the ribbon or cording to tie it with. Traditionally, three, seven or nine herbs in equal parts are added to a single bag.

PROTECTION – (white) ash, basil, bay, dill, fennel, mistletoe, mugwort, periwinkle, rosemary, rowan, st. john's wort, trefoil, vervain.

HEALING – (blue) garlic, eucalyptus, cinnamon, sage, saffron, sandalwood, lavender, rosemary, myrrh.

LOVE – (red) apple, coriander, dragon's blood, jasmine, lavender, mandrake, marjoram, rose, rosemary, vervain, yarrow.

WEALTH / PROSPERITY – (green) benzoin, cinnamon, patchouli, clove, sage, nutmeg, basil, dill.

RUNES

While many folk have recently lent their contributions to runic magick, the popular modern and public integration of Norse, Elven and Futhark Runes seems to have stemmed from the writing and personal research of J.R.R. Tolkein. Even prior to the New Age Movement in the 1960s, many people actually believed that Tolkein had invented them from scratch. Two decades ago, Ralph Blum produced the now famous "Rune Kit" (*Book of Runes*), which became the modern benchmark and an instant bestseller, bringing the symbolism of the runes to light for contemporary society. Now they appear everywhere and in all forms of media.

Modern practitioners use the Futhark Alphabet as a substitution or compliment to the magickal use of names and formulas. The Norse-Elven runes are most often used for "key word divination," but the runic tradition actually operates at a much deeper level.

The word "rune" is a Germanic term meaning, "secret" or "hidden," not altogether different than the Greek word, "occult" (and the Latin, "arcanum"). In other words, "runic magick" is the "secret magick," dealing with the realm of the "invisible" or Otherworld. Although most runic magicians uphold a tradition in the Norse flavor of Viking-pirates, the older Edaphic traditions maintain that the "Runes of Europe," both the Futhark and the Ogham, originated with the Elves, faerie folk and Dragon Kings. And while it is rarely recognized in the New Age, the more commonly used Futhark system has just as high of an affinity for Nature as the Ogham does.

Runes do, in fact, represent letters or characters of language, but wizards view words, sounds and tones on a more metaphysical level than are generally maintained in contemporary society. Alphabets (e.g. the Ogham and Enochian) are not intended for simply the writing of words derived from ever-changing thoughts. Divine Names and Hermetic formulas, such as the *Tetragrammaton* are "meta-words" that deserve

For spellcraft and talisman construction, the names of people, targets and goals are often written in mystical characters.

ᚠ	ᚢ	ᚦ	ᚨ	ᚱ	ᚲ
Fehu F	Uryz U	Thuryaz Th	Ansuz A	Raydo R	Kano C K
ᚷ	ᚹ	ᚺ	ᚾ	ᛁ	ᛃ
Gebo G	Wynjo W	Hagalz H	Nauthyz N	Isya I	Jyra J
ᛇ	ᛈ	ᛉ	ᛋ	ᛏ	ᛒ
Eihwaz Y	Pyrth P	Algyz X Z	Sowelu S	Teywaz T	Berkana B
ᛗ	ᛗ	ᛚ	ᛝ	ᛞ	ᛟ
Ehwaz E	Mannan M	Laguz L	Ynguz Y	Dagaz D	Uthyla O

The physical act of inscribing the runes, whether on talismans or by using a more formalized practice (Galdrostaffyr System), should be conducted as a sacred and magickal act, as is the final consecration of the item. Similar to the spells cast by sympathetic magick, the physical gestures and movements of "rune-casting" are representative of invisible (metaphysical) counter-parts. The wizard traces the rune for its symbolic pro-perties, using the action to project correlating vibrations of raised energy. The bind-runes are composite runes that combine more than one runic character to form a potent glyph. Depending on the needs of the practit-ioner, several runes may work well together and they can be combined to form a unique sigil for the particular operation.

FEHU - "F" prosperity, possessions,
    wealth, power
URUZ - "U" strength, manifestation,
    sacrifice
THURISA - "Th" destruction, defense,
    gateway, demons
ANSUZ - "A" signal, expression,
    reception, transformation
RAIDO - "R" right action, wagon,
    journey
KANO - "C" "K" opening, creativity,
    torch
GEBO - "G" partnership, sacrifice,
    magick, sexuality

WUNJO - "W" joy, harmony,
   fellowship
HAGALZ - "H" disruption, hail,
   framework
NAUTHIZ - "N" constraint,
   deliverance, persistence
ISA - "I" ice, concentration, standstill
JERA - "J" harvest, fertility, peace
EIHWAZ - "Y" defense, yew tree, life
   and death cycles
PERTH - "P" initiation, karma,
   assertiveness
ALGIZ - "X" "Z" protection, life,
   the Elf
SOWELU - "S" wholeness, sun,
   victory
TEIWAZ - "T" warrior, justice,
   god's judgment
BERKANA - "B" birth, life cycle,
   growth, birch tree
EHWAZ - "E" movement, the horse,
   soul travel
MANNAZ - "M" humans, intelligence,
   the self
LAGUZ - "L" flow, lake life, fertility
INGUZ - "Ng" fertility, power,
   potential, raw energy
DAGAZ - "D" day light, breakthroughs,
   prosperity

OTHILA - "O" property, prosperity, separations

PUTTING IT TOGETHER

Why are so many people drawn to spellcraft? Most likely it is because of the promises of material gain and power that it offers...the sorcerer is no exception, for there is obvious merit to using low magickal spellcraft.

But I warn those who practice the arts not to become obsessive or power hungry – and there are much deeper levels of magick and metaphysical spirituality available to the seeker – don't allow low magick to rule your life (and I speak from personal experience) – don't let the magick consume you in your naivete – but don't fear it either.

Also – be smart! If you have an SAT test, study! If you have a job interview, look your best! You can always use spellcraft to assist your life, but don't allow it to control or run it for you. That is not only a sign of great weakness but an abuse of the power.

Some sorcerers believe magick should be used

solely as a last resort – others believe that you only get so much in a single lifetime – still more hold the idea that magick ages the body prematurely (while the other half think it keeps you young).

You will also have personal reserves of energy and access to the external, and therefore always possess the means to tap the arts of spellcraft. The other myths were created by medieval sorcerers as vices to keep their apprentices from abusing the power. In truth, these ideas simply aren't valid. The only drawback is "wild magick" and "backfires" from the naïve and dabblers – so keep a pure and dedicated mind.

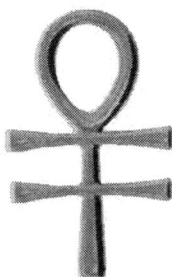

ELEMENTALISM

As we perceive them in the fragmented physical world, there appear to be four primary elements (plus a fifth of quintessence). Earth provides the sorcerer with structure, substance and foundation. They are the keys to abundance.

Air offers communication, illumination, focus and clarity; the codes of intellect. Fire gives strength, courage, vitality and faith, offering personal and external protection. Water brings transformation, healing and purity, the means to inner wisdom. Sounds pretty good, eh? So how does one go about tapping into this awesome spectrum of elemental powers? The sorcerer employs Elvish and Druidic practices.

ELEMENTAL MAGICK

The basic foundation of all practical Nature/ Earth-oriented systems of magick operating under the premise that knowledge of the "composition" of energy enables it to be used and transformed constructively. Although traditions vary concerning the quantity of elements and the divisions of the attributes, most of the non-chemical paradigms are based on the four basic currents: air, earth, fire and water. These forces, as well as metallic elements interpreted in the form of planetary energy, became the focus of ancient alchemy.

The material elements, earth and air, divide the basic interpretive division into solids and gasses. Water was later discovered to be composed of more elements and fire was rejected from the model as a "process" of combustion, not a standalone element.

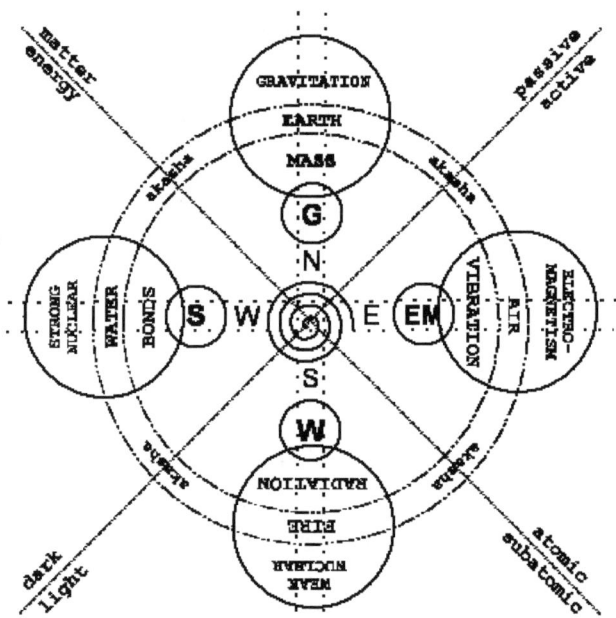

In the current author's personal model, earth and air correspond to the first two forms of manifestation that modern science becomes familiar with: gravity-G and electromagnetism-EM. The discovery of the other two subatomic nuclear forces completes the fourfold "stan-dard model" of Western Elementalism. In this model, fire corresponds to the W-weak (nuc-lear) force responsible for radiation, fusion and heat. The qualities found in the water element correspond to the S-strong (nuclear) force that bonds and unites particles together all across the fabric of space. This model has never before been presented in New Age literature.

Elemental magick is the basis for all practical systems used in the New Age. Every facet of virtually any philosophical, scientific or mag-ickal model can be reduced to an elemental relationship. Wizards who use such models in their interpretation of energy and existence are called "Elementalists." This passion can be found in most areas of quantum and particle physics today as well as the modern quests for the unification of the "standard model." Elem-entalists have already gained a sense of this unifying force in their own models, calling it Akasha, the essence of all things both manifest and invisible. It suggests a new vision for the "aether" as an inter-dimensional shroud or brane by which the elemental forces are able to vibrate their existence. This "fifth element" or spiritual dimension would in fact hold the sum of the other elements in it as well. This is why Akasha has the peculiar attribute of being a fifth "encompassing" element and yet the product of all four at the same time. This type of metaphysics is only discernible by adopting "dimensional theories."

For novices, elementalism can be a quite individual path of exploration. It requires that the student work with and understand the energy of each of the elements. Not only are physical manifestations of the elements employed, astral journeys and visualizations into the elemental realms or "domains" are also observed. When calling elementals to the ritual nemeton, these beings or conscious personifications of the energetic current, are visualized as coming to the edge of the circle. The wizard invites their energy into the nemeton via intention. Elemental tablets and candles (of an appropriate color) are set out at each of the four directions, each corresponding to a specific element. [In traditional interpretations these are north-earth, east-air, south-fire and west-water.] The correspondences of the elements can be envisioned coherently in a circle that also corresponds to other forms of magickal timing, including seasonal and daily phases.

SIGNS OF PORTAL

The Druids perceived basic geometric forms as being tied to the elements. They can be traced in the air with an appropriate tool or the power finger in an appropriate elemental color.

The earth glyph is a representation of a stone trilithon, such as is seen at megalithic sites like Stonehenge. The air sign is a an equal-armed cross of the four winds. The fire triangle is symbolic of mountain-tops and flame, note that in chemistry it becomes the sign of "chemical change." And finally the water sign is a concave reflective of the inward slope of a cup or the water's surface between wave peaks.

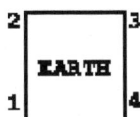

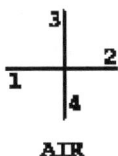

ELEMENTAL TABLETS

The basic elemental forces that bind existence together are represented in traditions of ceremonial magick with "tablets" set out at the four corners (directions) of the nemeton.

AIR   FIRE

The more intricate the system of magick, the more complex the tablet

EARTH   WATER

design is. [Enochian Tablets are a perfect example.] Basic ones can be constructed from wood or cardboard for effective ritual magick and spellcraft. The most basic glyphs used are the ancient Hermetic-Alchemical symbols for the elements.

ELEMENTAL BEINGS

Sorcerers believe in the conscious or intelligent energies that possess characteristics based on the "element" (air, earth, fire and water) they are created from. The term "elemental" can also relate to anything pertaining to the elements themselves or the philosophy and practice of elemental magick. The sentient beings exist in elemental domains or kingdoms that are wrapped in the unseen dimensions. Elementals possess both material and metaphysical properties, including the ability to travel (transition) between dimensions.

According to the Edaphic (Elven) Tradition the "elementals" have the ability to mate with humans when in material form, something that *has* happened, causing the creation of the faerie folk that were driven under-ground with the rise of human populations during the Dark Ages. Elemental blood still exists in some corners of the genetic pool. These metaphysical beings also have the ability to "walk-in" to an existing material body (simulacrum) through a process called transignation.

Elementals appear in all global mythologies, now perceived as "creatures of fantasy." The attitude taken by most New Age practitioners is that these beings are not "imaginary" in the sense of being fictitious, but their energetic memory is, for the most, confined to the Astral Plane or Otherworld. Given the interconnectedness-unification of all elements, physical and spiritual dimensions, these conscious currents of energy can be reached from the mind or nemeton.

In ritual, Elemental beings are summoned to lend their energy to your working. In essence, the Elementals are the perspective of the observer capable of perceiving the energetic currents. The preexisting beings are composed of one element with additional affinities to others possible, though wizards of alchemy use the energetic currents and rays of light to form or manifest (new) intelligences (elementary beings) for their specific purposes.

Inter-dimensional and elemental beings are one of the most difficult aspects of magick to conceive of from a world of conditioned "rational" thought. The simple explanation is that the ritualized elementals are a projection from the consciousness of the operator made tangible by the energetic belief accumulated from thousands of years of elemental magick being practiced on the Earth. The archetypal memory that remains can continue to be fed more energy over time, provided that the traditions continue to be observed. Grimoires such as the *Keys of Solomon*, depict a different picture. According to these medieval wizards, the intelligences are emanated or given substance by a natural elemental phenomenon existent in the Universe. Whether clouds, fire or the rays of the Sun, the wizards and mystics of

104

the ages have perceived the energy to be intelligent and dynamic, not merely static.

The pantheistic view of the Universe has led most cowans to misinterpret the metaphysical philosophy of thresholds. The act of rain, in and of itself, is not believed to be intelligent or alive. What the rain provides is an energetic polarized elemental charge that causes a space to possess a greater affinity towards a particular energy and is somehow entangled to it. This then cases the threshold phenomenon to reson-ate with a specific spiritual intelligence, simply *called* "rain-spirits" by indigenous shamans.

By the Hermetic axiom, "as above, so below," and many other reactive/correspondence princ-iples that the metaphysical paradigm as a whole, suggest, there is a constant relationship between physical phenomenon and spiritual or meta-physical energy. In ritual and other ceremonial magick, the wizard observes this principle in efforts to bring the nemeton to a state or freq-uency that resonates with the energy sought.

ABSORBING TREE ENERGY

The Druids were well learned in tapping into

the energy of trees. Using "Oghamic" and other tree lore, the sorcerer might also wish to tap into the energies of certain trees based on their attributes. This type of working can also be performed to aid in restoring a personal cache of energy and to increase stamina (endurance).

*go to a special tree (pine tree for
    beginners)
*touch your fingers to the sharp needle
    ends
*hold for at least three minutes
*visualize a green-white stream of
    energy flowing from the tree
    to you.

RITE OF THREE RAYS

This working is a Druidic-Gnostic-Hermetic invocation using the "hidden name", IAO. It is similar to other preliminary rituals such as the "pentagram rite". The radiance of the "divine rays" is often depicted by a three sharp lines.

The key to success is to gauge your breath in such a way as to allow your hands to reach your sides just as you have emptied your breath.

*begin meditative breathing
*take a deep breath, raise your arms
*let your hands come down to your
    sides, intoning: "**I**" ("**eee**")
*inhale, raising hands, exhale,
    intoning: "**A**" ("**ahh**")
*inhale, raising hands, exhale,
    intoning: "**O**" ("**ohh**")
*do again, combining the forms,
    intoning: "**IAO**"

POLARITY OF POWER

The Druids classified their magick according to the "Elven Rays" - from this we have classification terms like "black magick" and "white magick". But there is, in actuality, an entire spectrum between and also none, for all in existence comes from the singular light.

> RED – physical, healing, passion
> ORANGE – courage, pride, heroism
> YELLOW – alchemy, meditation,
>   intellect
> GREEN – nature, herbalism, fertility
> BLUE – emotional, love, peace
> PURPLE – psychical, psionic, spiritual
> WHITE – blessing, healing, non-
>   physical
> BLACK – blight, curses, hexes, bindings

ELEMENTAL WEAPONS

The original representations of the forces of Nature or "elements" were actually weapons of warfare that eventually became mystical relics. Historically, elemental magick emerged from the practices of the Elves, faerie folk and Dragon Kings who were performing the operations taught to them from the *Anunnaki* and their earthly descendents. The traditional form adopted today is derived from the Celtic and Druid cycles, also originating in Mesopotamia by way of the Tuatha d'Anu. Today, some archaic traditions of ceremonial magick (esp. the Golden Dawn System) still refer to the ritual tools as "elemental weapons."

108

The actual tool or representative object used will differ with the tradition observed. The original "Gifts of Faerie" are very closely connected to the elemental currents and members of the Tuatha d'Anu. In high and ceremonial magick that is closely aligned with the Hebrew-Kabbalah, each tool or weapon represents a letter of the Tetragrammaton also supplemented in ritual with elemental tablets. Consequently, the sword actually exists as a separate entity in the Golden Dawn System, which adopts the wand for the fire element and an athame for air.

In the system of elemental magick adopted by the Tuatha d'Anu, the Sword of Nuada represents the fire element. Usually a blade of some kind, even a sickle, ritually represents fire, though a seeker will also find evidence of alternate practices. The Spear of Lugh symbolizes the air element, often substituted with a wand in most modern traditions. The water element corresponds to the Cauldron of the Dagda, which is sometimes depicted as a chalice or "grail." Finally, the pentacle or earthstone is based on the Stone of Fal or "dragonstone." Many representations have been derived from these symbols during the evolution of the Western Magickal Tradition.

INFLUENCING OTHERS

The magick used to manipulate others to see in your favor – personal magnetism... as wrong as this might seem to some, sometimes people need a good kick, eh? The following working is to be performed before retiring for the evening, which will enable your subconscious mind to work its own magick. Remember that people are often more receptive when they are sleeping.

*lie comfortably on your back
*progressively relax the whole body
*use meditative breathing for three to
      five minutes
*intone the name "IAO" (properly...)
      three times
*visualize the person you wish to
      influence
*merge their astral form with yours
*feel as if you are becoming this person
*hold this image for three to five minutes
*think of the thoughts/images you want
      them to have
*think for that person, using "I"
      repeatedly
*abruptly dismiss the visualization and
      ground

110

TREE COMMUNICATION

The Druids acknowledged that all life had a spiritual energy to it – and with trees, well, Druids recognized them as tremendous store-houses of natural power and even as living libraries of earth memory. The following app-roach is simple, but time-proven.

*go to a special or sacred tree
*sit close, legs crossed, arms out-
      stretched touching the tree
*begin meditative breathing
*progressively relax the whole body
*speak clearly to the tree from your
      spirit:
    Spirit of the sacred tree
    Make yourself known to me
    I invoke you for the sake of speech
    And wish to learn all you will teach.
*spread your palms wide over the bark
      of the tree
*visualize green life-force energy
      leaving your hands
*see white energy coming back and
      forming above your head.

When the tree is ready it will project imagery into the cloud formed above your head. Trees communicate using graphics and beginners may even only see colors. This is something that is extremely safe and rewarding for increased experimentation on the part of the sorcerer.

TREE RITUAL

A basic tree ritual can be expanded as the sorcerer sees fit. These rituals are actually of the second degree of the Druids, the Ovydd grade, pertaining specifically to trees and Nature. Begin your ritual by making a formal invocation, touching the tree and essentially performing a "tree communication". Evoke the spirits of the tree by intoning their names in as many tongues as you can. The following list was taken from the Ogham tables.

> BIRCH – beith – boibel
> ROWAN – luis – loth
> ALDER – fearn – forann
> WILLOW – saille – saliath
> ASH – nuin – nebagadon
> HAWTHORN – huatha – huria
> OAK – duir – daibuheeth
> HOLLY – tinne – teilmon
> HAZEL – coll – cae
> APPLE – quert – qaylip

112

VINE – muin – muriath
IVY – gort – gahth
REED – nehtahl – nomahr
BLACKTHORN – straif – stru
ELDER – ruis – ruiben
FIR – ailim – achab
FURZE – ohn – oise
HEATHER – ur – urith
ASPEN – eadhe – essu
YEW – ioho – iachim

Finally, make the benediction by knocking on the bark of the tree three times. Doing regular practices like these will not only increase your "authority" with Nature, but also your kinship with trees and the forests.

ELEMENTAL RITUAL

This solitary ritual is based on the British Druid Tradition. Go to a ritual nemeton outdoors and set up a stone circle using your own height as the diameter. Be sure to bring your Elemental Tools with you and lay them at the proper quarters of your circle.

Go to the centre of your nemeton and say:

I stand on a threshold between worlds at a time that is not a time, in a place that is not a place, on a day that is not a day, between the worlds and beyond, yet I am here. I who occupy this sacred centre is at one with many gods who are but faces of the One God. I claim the right for this moment outside of time to be a God myself.

Go to the north and take a pinch of seal-salt and sprinkle some onto your tongue, then take another pinch and sprinkle it onto the ground. Trace the Earth Sign of Portal with the stone and say:

I invoke you O powers of the Earth, the kingdom of Stone. I call out to the kingdom of Falias, Ghobas and Morfessas. Hear my call. Hear my call. I summon your infinite powers. Come forth from the North that you shall be known.

Go to the east and take a handful of petals from a rose to scatter in the air and let them float to the ground. Using the air tool, trace the Air Sign of Portal and say:

I invoke you O powers of the Air, the kingdom of Wind. I call out to the kingdom of Esras, Gorias and Paraldas. Hear my call. Hear my call. I summon your infinite powers. Come forth from the East that you shall be known.

Go to the south and burn a special Druidic incense mixture of mistletoe and oak. Trace the Fire Sign of Portal with the sickle or blade, saying:

I invoke you O powers of Fire, the kingdom of Flame. I call out to the kingdom of the Flames of Consciousness, the kingdom of Finias, Uscias and Djinas. Hear my call. Hear my call. I summon your infinite powers. Come forth from the South that you shall be known.

Go to the west and pour a libation or some water from your chalice or cup. Trace the Water Sign of Portal with the water tool, saying:

I invoke you O powers of Water, the kingdom of the Sea, I call out to the kingdom of the Waves of the Subconsciousness, the kingdom of Mur-ias, Semias and Niksas. Hear my call. Hear my call. I summon your infinite powers. Come forth from the West that you shall be known.

Return to the centre of the circle and say:

Elemental spirits of the outer realms – bless,

guard and shield me always. Around me and within me, above and below me. Protect me from myself and others. I declare by the strength of the Elder Gods, the Great Ideals of the mysteries and the highest heights of the Guardians of the Universe.

The ritual is completed. If desired, other magickal workings can be performed within this consecration of sacred space (nemeton – mandala). From the elementalist standard, this would be a more advanced magickal operation for "casting the circle" then has been dis-cussed previously.

MODERN SORCERERS

THE GOLDEN DAWN

Considered the most famous and influential magickal secret society to grace modern civilization, the "Hermetic Order of the Golden Dawn" (GD) was founded in 1895 by Free-masons and Rosicrucians. The Order went on to attract many well-known mystics like W.B. Yeats, Arthur Edward Waite, Israel Regardie and Aleister Crowley.

The GD system of apprenticeship consists of 10+1 grades of study based on the stations (sephiroth) of the Kabbalah.

> 0-0: Neophyte
> 1-10: Zelator (Malkuth/earth)
> 2-9: Theoricus (Yesod/air)
> 3-8: Practicus (Hod/water)
> 4-7: Philsophus (Netzach/fire)
> 5-6: Adeptus Minor (Tiphareth/harmony)
> 6-5: Adeptus Major (Geburah/might)
> 7-4: Adeptus Exemptus (Chesed/mercy)
> 8-3: Magister Templi (Binah/
>   understanding)

9-2: Magus (Chokmah/wisdom)
10-1: Ipsissimis (Kether/Akasha)

The origin of the Golden Dawn is somewhat of a mystery. Some believe it was originally a revival or chapter of a very secret German Order, possibly the Saturnalian Illuminati. Most believe that the ceremonies of the grades (initiations) are based on obscure manuscripts of Freemason and/or Rosicrucian origins. In fact, the very "vault" used as a "ritual chamber" for secret ceremonial observation in GD is based on the tomb of Christian Rosenkreutz, a seven-sided room with each section of wall being five feet wide and eight feet from floor to ceiling. The legend of Rosenkreutz is a part of the Rosicrucian legacy, however, to give the GD some legitimacy, his body *was* found with a book of rites and ceremonies, and on the cover, a "T" with an intertwined serpent.

S.L. MACGREGOR MATHERS

The wizard usually associated with the founding and running of the original Golden Dawn is known as MacGregor Mathers. The practical GD teachings were heavily based on the grimoires and manuscripts Mathers translated himself, most famously: the *Keys of Solomon* and the *Sacred Book of Magick of Abramelin the Mage*. Higher degrees of the GD focused on the Kabbalah and Enochian Magick embedded within these grimoires. The emphasis on mysticism and magick is what attracted the "would-be wizards" to approach the Great Work from a practical paradigm rather than the more philosophical traditions of Freemasonry. This later became known as the "Golden Dawn System of Magic."

ALEISTER CROWLEY

Perhaps the most famous member of the GD, Aleister Crowley, never was allowed initiation to the Inner Circle of the Order. This was a wise decision by the Order since Crowley published the secret Outer Court tradition to cowans of the GD.

When Mathers refused to "see him through" to the higher degrees, Crowley retaliated with magickal warfare. Eventually, both were unseated from the GD and W.B. Yeats went on to run it in Mathers absence. Following a schism in the Order in 1903, A.E. Waite went on to form his own Order, the "Holy Order of the

Golden Dawn." Many members followed Waite. Some went on to form the Stella Matutina (SM). With the loss of so many high-ranking and leading personalities (and the additional loss of secrecy, thanks to Crowley) the integrity of the original Order began to fall.

THE GOLDEN DUSK

One unique aspect about the Order is that Mathers claimed a "Third Circle" existed, which only those Ascended Masters who were consulted on the Astral Plane were initiated into. Prior to his excommunication, Mathers said that he had personally been initiated into this degree, which caused many members to begin to question his validity, or worse, his sanity. Further, when Crowley condemned the GD to death by publishing their secrets, he said he did so under the direction of the "Secret Chiefs" or "Inner Plane Adepti."

After Crowley published his own version of the GD materials, Israel Regardie felt obligated to clarify the matter. He republished all the original GD materials in four volumes, titled simply *The Golden Dawn*. He later compiled a more readable version called *The Complete Sys-*

tem of Golden Dawn Magic. While the organization is now a feint shadow of what it once was, many modern magicians attempt to self-initiate themselves into the tradition. The richness and symbolism of the ceremonies, reminiscent of those of Freemasonry, have been considered outdated by many modern practitioners in the New Age. The sheer bulk and crypticism of the GD methods is enough to turn many away, not to mention numerous occult errors, the system-method still holds many valid contributions.

A.E. WAITE

Arthur Edward Waite was one of the most prestigious members of the Hermetic Order of the Golden Dawn (GD) and an initiate of the "Inner Order" (or "Second Order"). A.E. Waite was considered the authoritative scholar on ceremonial magick along with the later rival for the title, Israel Regardie (also a member of GD), after Aleister Crowley was excommunicated and Mac-Gregor Mathers is unseated from his position as the head of the "Second Order." In 1903, William Butler Yeats (yes, the famed poet) replaces Mathers and Waite decides to leave to form his own branch of the "Second

Order." He kept with the GD traditions, calling his secret society the "Ordo Rosae Rubae et Aureae Crucis" (R.R. et A.C.), translating to "The Order of the Ruby Red Rose and Golden Cross" or "rosy-cross" ["rose cross" root: Rosicrucian - "rosae cruces"]. Waite rewrote many of the original GD rites of initiation and other operations for his order.

The most famous public contribution of Arthur Edward Waite is the Rider-Waite tarot deck, perhaps the best-selling and most quickly recognizable version of the tarot, based on the GD symbolism coupled with lore from alchemical schools and the Kabbalah.

A.E. Waite also wrote *The Pictorial Key to the Tarot* (1910), which like his deck, is still the best-selling book on the topic of tarot.

In 1898 he released *The Book of Black Magick and Pacts*, which was later reprinted more accurately as *The Complete Grimoire* and *The Complete Book of Ceremonial Magick*. The book extracts verbatim excerpts and explains the magick of many now-popular grimoires for the first time publicly. It influenced everyone from Aleister Crowley to Gerald Gardner and Alex Sanders (Wicca), bringing to light that which had only been known prior to initiates of GD.

As a result, Waite is considered a significant influence for the increased use of "ceremonial magick" in mainstream occultism.

TAROT OF THE GOLDEN DAWN

Lore suggests that the modern French word "tarot" is derived from "tarocchi," an Italian plural form of "tarocco" meaning "trump." The twenty-two cardinal archetypes of the "Major Arcana" are often referred to as "trumps." The word "tarotee" describes the cross-hatch line pattern that graced the card-backs of most early decks. The "Minor Arcana" is the precursor to the modern "playing card" decks, which can also be used as an oracle.

The trump cards of the primary archetypes are superior to the remainder of the deck and may be effectively studied and used independent of the others. Their symbolism has been connected to Jungian archetypes, alchemy, the kabbalah and the journey of the spirit to wholeness or enlightenment (via the Right Way to Ascension). Regardless of whether or not the ancient

Egyptians and Hermeticists actively used a "tarot card" system, the GD and its members researched and wrote hundreds of pages of discourses providing interpret-ations and ritual correspondences.

In addition to "Gypsy Divination," as they call it, they use the Major Arcana for pathworking (focusing/meditating on the symbolism of a card to trigger certain astral visions). Some operations suggest meditating on a card before sleeping and then placing it under you pillow to inspire lucid-dreaming.

The symbolism of the tarot has received an interpretation into every theme and flavor imaginable. That is the beauty of universal archetypes: they apply to everything. Even the Ogham, a completely independent system with more recently ascribed oracular aspects, shares direct synchronicity with the Major Arcana. With all of the decks available on the market, few practitioners are actually aware of the "original" GD sets that the others have been based on.

Arthur Edward Waite commissioned artist Pamela Colman Smith to graphically depict the tarot to the specifications put forth by the GD discourses and his own analysis of Hermetic lore. The deck's release accompanied his most famous book, *The Pictorial Key to the Tarot* (1910), both of which were produced by Rider publications and hence the name: Rider-Waite Tarot. When the famous GD schism occurred in the early 20th Century, Aleister Crowley went on to create his own deck, dedicated to "Thoth" (Hermes). Israel Regardie created another deck, which did not gain significant exposure until the tarot craze of the 1980s (mainly due to a popular James Bond movie that actually had a deck commissioned specifically for it – now sold to the public as "Tarot of the Witches").

The Major Arcana should be the focus of the current seeker. Those cards are numbered "0" to "21" and have titled names, easily separable from the rest of the pack. The symbolism provided here is from the Hermetic sources that originally prompted the New Age interest but have since been mainly ignored.

In addition to the archetypal symbolism more commonly equated to the Major Arcana trumps, the Golden Dawn System corr-elates both astrological significance and the "paths" of the Kabbalah. The "paths" connect the ten "sephir-oth," "spheres" or "stations" of the Kabbalah.

125

Each of the Kabbalistic pathways vibrates a multi-ray frequency that can be used in work beyond divination.

As with all oracular systems, the operator must become familiarized with the symbols and symbolism prior to their practical use. This can even require equating a different association with a card than what is provided here. The system must be personalized to be effective. Spend time meditating on each of the card (variables) and their attributes by themselves. Afterward, you can integrate them together into a coherent system.

The Major Arcana

0 – FOOL: Crown of Wisdom, the arts of divination and the "Primary Universal Motion" acting through the air element on the zodiac.
    -Keywords: crossroads, decisions, new beginnings and taking measure before acting.

1 – MAGICIAN: Crown of Understanding, the arts of healing and the "Prima Materia" acting through (philosophic) Mercury onto Saturn.
    -Keywords: application of willpower and

ability, learning and use of knowledge.

2 – HIGH PRIESTESS: Crown of Beauty, the abilities of clairvoyance (spirit vision) and the "Primum Mobile" acting though the Moon onto the Sun.
    -Keywords: inspiration, intuition, spiritual connection and uncovering hidden influences.

3 – EMPRESS: Wisdom of Understanding, the arts and experience of love and the Sphere of the Zodiac acting through Venus on Saturn.
    -Keywords: fertility, growth, joy, prosperity and satisfaction.

4 – EMPEROR: Wisdom of Beauty, acts of consecration and the Sphere of the Zodiac acting through Aries on the Sun (the beginning of the spring season).
    -Keywords: exterior authority, inner balance, responsibility and use of experience.

5 – HIGH PRIEST (HIEROPHANT): Wisdom of Mercy, the ability to summon inner strength and the Sphere of the Zodiac acting through Taurus on Jupiter.
    -Keywords: open-mindedness or stubb-

ornness (reversed), recognition of truth and solidifying foundations.

6 – LOVERS: Understanding of Beauty, the gift of prophecy and Saturn acting through Gemini on the Sun.
-Keywords: changes, determination, possible indication of relationship and love.

7 – CHARIOT: Understanding of Strength (Severity), the magick of enchantment and Saturn acting through Cancer onto Mars.
-Keywords: application of energy, movement, self-discipline, travel, triumph and success in a cycle.

8 – STRENGTH: Mercy of Strength (Severity), the ability to temper the wild nature of animals or men and Jupiter acting through Leo onto Mars.
-Keywords: disillusionment, need for organization, use of personal strength and the assurance of success if temperance is exercised.

9 – HERMIT: Mercy of Beauty, the arts of invisibility and Jupiter acting through Virgo on the Sun.

-Keywords: experimentation, guidance, responsibility, true wisdom and withdrawal.

10 – WHEEL OF FORTUNE: Mercy of Victory, the Right Way and Jupiter acting directly onto Venus.
-Keywords: chance, cycles, opportunity, randomness and the ups and downs of life.

11 – JUSTICE: Strength (Severity) of Beauty, guiding justice and Mars acting through the Scale of Libra on the Sun.
-Keywords: consideration of all factors, equality, fairness and possible external influences.

12 – HANGED MAN: Strength (Severity) of Glory/ Splendor, the use of talismans and Mars acting through the water element onto Mercury.
-Keywords: changing directions, the need for foresight, indecision, transitions ("mid-life crisis") and self-sacrifice.

13 – DEATH: Beauty of Victory, the arts of necromancy and the Sun acting through Scorpio on Venus.
-Keywords: abrupt change, letting go,

transition and unfortunate realizations.

14 – TEMPERANCE (BALANCE): Beauty of Foundation, alchemy or transmutation and the Sun acting through Sagittarius on the Moon.
>-Keywords: execute balance, seek security and harmony, slow down and temper your emotions.

15 – DEVIL (HORNED ONE): Beauty of Glory (False Splendor), the use of the evil eye and the Sun acting through Capricorn onto Mercury.
>-Keywords: arrogance, bondage, egotism, pride, materialism and the need for self-control.

16 – TOWER (FALLING TOWER): Victory of Glory (Splendor), the use of curses for revenge and Venus acting through Mars upon Mercury.
>-Keywords: breakdown, clinging to the old, false hopes and sudden changes.

17 – STARS: Victory of the Foundation (Fundamental World), the use of true astrology and Venus acting through Aquarius on the Moon.
>-Keywords: future accomplishments, high hopes, ideals, and the need for clarity and spiritual aid.

18 – MOON: Victory of the Kingdom (Material World), the practice of elemental magick or glamourie and Venus acting through Pisces onto the priori elemental forces.

> -Keywords: dreams, hidden influences/ forces, intuition needed, self-reliance required and subtle changes to come.

19 – SUN: Glory (Splendor) of the Kingdom (Material World), the use of grimoires or evocation and Mercury acting through the Sun onto the Moon.

> -Keywords: blessings, brightness, brilliance, fulfillment, happiness, honesty, joy and laughter.

20 – JUDGMENT: Glory (Splendor) of the Foundation (Spiritual Realm), the use of wealth magick and Mercury acting through Fire (possibly Akasha) on the cosmic elements.

> -Keywords: completion near, forth- coming renewal, guidance needed, looking ahead and an observation period.

21 – UNIVERSE (WORLD): The Foundation (Fundamental Level) of the Kingdom (Material World), all natural Earth-oriented magick (geo- mancy, Ogham, etc.).

> -Keywords: cycle ends, freedom, perfect-

ion, satisfaction, success and triumph.

The card deck is cut and shuffled by the operator. Some cards are occasionally allowed to fall (this usually happens anyways), which are then put back into the deck "reversed" so that some cards may be placed upside-down in a spread with the figures standing on their heads. These cards are interpreted as the anti-thesis of what has been described for them prior or else indicative of an extreme need to acquire such qualities. Some practitioners simply cut the deck, reverse half of the cards, and then continue shuffling.

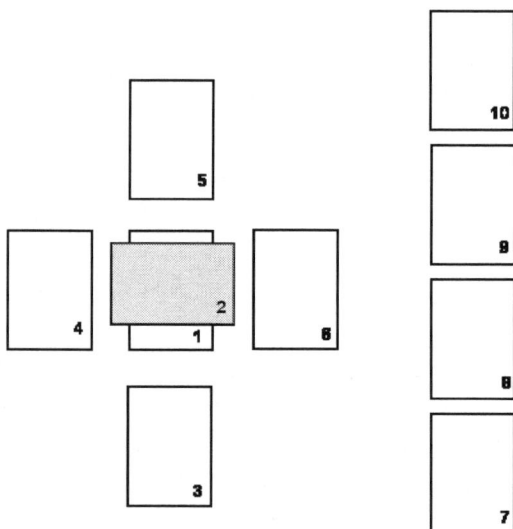

The most common "spread" or "layout" for the tarot is known as the ten-card Celtic or Gypsy method. It was also taught in the Golden Dawn System. This method requires placing ten randomly drawn cards in a predetermined pattern or spread. The operator or "reader" posses the question and begins drawing each card one by one while reading or stating the function of each card. At the end, all cards are interpreted both individually and in relation to one another.

1. "This envelops you." This card represents the observer of the question, the general atmosphere, aura or personal influence.

2. "This blocks you." This card represents the forces of opposition acting against the particular situation. This is the primary barrier to success.

3. "This is beneath you," representing the basic foundation, or that which is already evident or can be energetically drawn from as a resource.

4. "This is behind you," representing the influences or forces that have passed into the past, including experience that can be energetically drawn from as a resource.

5. "This crowns you." This card shows the evident overt ideals, goals or aims of the situation. It represents the energy that you are or should be drawing "down."

6. "This is before you," representing the direct action forthcoming and the near-future influences that can be energetically drawn from as a resource.

7. "This is your true persona," reflective of how you should present yourself to others and carry yourself in the given situation (the true attitude or beliefs that becomes evident or covertly recognized).

8. "This is your house," depicting how others perceive you. This card also reflects you social self, the external influence that others (and your environment) project onto you.

9. "This is your hopes and fears," reflected in the symbolism of that will ultimately become evident, but first requires right thought and right action (see Right Way).

10. "This is the final result." This card not only gives the ultimate outcome of the situation (given the current movement of energy and

forces,) but it can also direct the reader's attention to other key cards that display what needs to change in order to change a given result. The outcome shows only the probably movement of energy if the given vibrational current continues to follow its given direction toward manifestation.

DID YOU KNOW ???

When the *Sorcerer's Handbook* premiered in 1998, the first edition, first printing had been printed from an old-fashioned typewriter. It was originally printed and bound by a local Denver printer until they decided to actually read it... then they refused to bind it anymore. After circulating in the underground for a few months, a second edition was printed exclusive-ly for members of the Elven Fellowship Circle of Magick and the Order of the Crystal Dawn. This followed with a third edition that was picked up by Abyss Distribution / Azure Green from 1998 until 2000 when it went out of print. A small print run of fourth and fifth editions were eventually made in anticipation of *Merl-yn's Magick*, and a sixth edition was released in 2009 exclusively to Mardukite Chamberlains.

MAGICK OF THE ORDER

THE MIDDLE PILLAR

The ritual of the middle pillar is one that all initiates of the Golden Dawn are initially instructed on. In the high magickal paradigm there are three pillars (sometimes called "rays" in other systems) and this exercise allows the sorcerer to assume the functional energy of the "middle pillar" - the crystalline pillar – that which balances the polarities of extremes viewed as the golden masculine pillar of severity and the silver feminine pillar of mercy. It is that balancing force that "Merlyn Stone's Order of the Crystal Dawn" is based.

> *close your eyes facing west
> *see the white pillar of severity on your
>   right
> *see the black pillar of mercy on your
>   left
> *imagine yourself as the middle pillar
>   between them
> *reflect/balance the powers/forces of the
>   two pillars
> *use meditative breathing

*raise your awareness above your head
*intone: *eh-heh-eh*
*imagine light descending from your
    head to neck
*intone: *yod-heh-vahv-heh ehl-oh-heem*
*imagine light descending from you neck
    to spine
*intone: *shah-dye el chye*
*imagine the light descend to your pelvic
    region
*intone: *ah-doh-nye hah-ah-retz*
*feel the light descend to your feet
*intone: *mahl-kuth*

The key to success for this rite is to allow the radiant light to descend slowly and wash throughout the whole body, being completely aware of its location as it moves. Each time the light reaches one of the "light centers", feel it swell up into a ball of light. Doing this effectively may cause an intoxicating flush sensation, but try to "feel" beyond simply the physical.

This working is also effective for accessing the "body of light" that is often alluded to in many traditions and systems of mysticism. Most high and ceremonial magick requires that the sorcerer enter the "body of light" prior to the actual working – and just to be sure, they instilled the means to do so in the preliminaries of their magickal workings. By dismissing the physical body and world, the sorcerer has the potential to momentarily "become more than human".

THE KABBALISTIC CROSS

This working appears in the preliminaries of most rites of the Golden Dawn and can be considered a form of self-blessing and for protection. The cross represents the balances and equilibrium of forces, specifically the four material directions (elements, etc.). Some init-iates are instructed to use a dagger or wand for this, but I have found that the index finger of the power hand works just as well.

*go to the east
*touch your forehead
*intone: *ah-tah*
*touch your breast
*intone: *mahl-kuth*
*touch your right shoulder
*intone: *veh-geh-boo-rah*
*touch your left shoulder
*intone: *lee-oh-lahm*
*clasp your hands at the chest
*intone: *ah-mon*

Those readers with a background in Judeo-Christian lore will recognize both the symbolism (the sign of the cross) and the statement made in Hebrew, which was at one time attached to the Lord's Prayer as a "standard" until relatively recently, translating to:

Power. Kingdom. Glory. Forever. Amen.

L.B.R.P

One of the most famous applications of the magick of the Order of the Golden Dawn is the "Lesser Banishing Ritual of the Pentagram" or L.B.R.P. It actually a minor rite among the many preliminaries found in the ceremonial liturgies – and it is also found again at the end of the same rites.

Essentially, the L.B.R.P. banishes the existing energies of place – the "spirit of the space" - during the consecration of a magick circle (as a means of "casting a circle" in high magick – just as we have seen in the elementalist styles and the basic styles given prior). It can also be used to negate the resonant energies leftover at the end of a ceremony.

The pentagram traced is always the "banishing form of earth":

It is visualized as blue in color.

When the center is pointed to, feel the pentagram as being "activated" - and burning brighter than before. The blue current is an emanation of the blue ray of protection. Carry the point to the next pentagram as you move about the circle in a clockwise motion addressing each direction.

*the ritual begins in the eastern quarter
*perform the Kabbalistic Cross Rite
*trace the pentagram, point to center and
        intone: *YHVH* ("*Yod-Heh-Vahv-
        Heh*")
*go to the south
*trace the pentagram, point to center and
        intone: *Adonai* ("*Ah-doh-nye*")
*do the same in the west, intoning
        "*Eh-heh-yeh*"

141

*and in the north, intone:
   Agla ("*Ah-glah*")
*carry your blue ray of light back to the
   east
*stand with arms outstretched and say:
   Before me: Raphael.
   Behind me: Gabriel.
   At my right hand: Michael.
   At my left hand: Oriel.
   Before me flames the pentagram.
   Above and below me shines the
      six-rayed star.

THE WATCHTOWER CEREMONY

Considered a supreme method of casting a
circle in the high magickal tradition. It is also
useful for all grimoire experimentation (including Enochian and other obscure forms of
ceremonial magick). The "Watchtower Ceremony," also called the "Watchtower Formulae,"
is used synonymously as a "formula of evocation" by the Golden Dawn.

The nemeton is arranged with a double circle
and the enochian tablets (or some form of
elemental tablet) is placed between the two
circles at their appropriate direction. A banner

can be used in place of the tablets. If being used for enochian magick, the appropriate enochian tools should be present.

*perform the Kabbalistic Cross Rite
*perform the L.B.R.P.
*stand in the south and raise your sword, saying:

Behold, all the phantoms have vanished and I see before me that sacred and formless fire that flames and consumes the hidden depths of the Universe and I hear the voice of the fire.

*feel and see the sword radiate with fire, and say:

Oh-ee-peh Teh-ah-ah Peh-doh-key [OIP TEAA PDOKE]. In the names and letters of the Great Southern Quadrangle, I invoke thee spirits of the Watchtower of the South.

*go to the west and take up the sacred chalice
*sprinkle some of the water, saying:

Now therefore I, a priest of fire, summon

143

the lustral waters of the sea and hear the wrath of the waves upon the shore, the voice of the water now and evermore.

*feel the water element rising up within
          you
*then say:

Em-pehheh Ar-ess-el Gah-ee-oh-leh [MPH ARSL GAIOL]. In the names and letters of the Great Western Quadrangle, I invoke thee spirits of the Watchtower of the West.

*go to the east and raise your dagger (or
          wand)
*strike the air three times saying:

My mind extends through the realm of air. In the formless air comes the vision and the voice, flashing, bounding, revolving, it whirls forth crying aloud.

*feel and see the winds of the air element
          swirling about you as you say:

Ohroh Ee-bah Ah-oh-zod-pee [ORO IBAH AOZPI]. In the names and letters of the Great Eastern Quadrangle, I

144

invoke thee spirits of the Watchtower of the East.

*go to the north and take up the pentacle
*shake it in the air three times and say:

I stoop down into a world of darkness, wherein lies unknown depths and Hades shrouded in gloom, delighting in senseless images; a black ever-rolling abyss, a voice both mute and void.

*feel the Earth beneath your feet
*become very aware of the ground as
        you intone:

Moh-are Dee-ah-leh Heh-keh-teh-gah [MOR DIAL HCTGA]. In the names and letters of the Great Northern Quad-rangle, I invoke thee spirits of the Watchtower of the North.

*go to the east and proclaim:

Holy art thou, Lord of the Universe. Holy art thou, whom Nature has not formed. Holy art thou, the Infinite and Mighty One, Lord of Light and of Darkness.

DID YOU KNOW ???

Of all the "Merlyn Stone / Joshua Free" books to date it is the *Sorcerer's Handbook* that has actually had the widest circulation from the underground, reaching thousands! The main portion of the 2005 release of *Merlyn's Magick* was actually based on the *Sorcerer's Handbook* and it went onto inspire other works such as *Arcanum* or *Magick & Mysticism*.

Following the release of the third edition and the plentiful demand in 1999, several shorter discourses were released as companions including: *The Young Sorcerer, Crystalline Awakening, Akasha, Necronomicon* and *Druid's Bible* – all of which were re-edited into the *Merlyn's Magick* anthology.

These titles all quickly went out-of-print by 2001 and were selling in the collectible markets for twice what they retailed for years before the release of *Merlyn's Magick*. Then, in 2001, "Merlyn Stone" disappeared.

In 2005, *Merlyn's Magick* was released by a third party under the authorship of "Joshua Free" compiling the works of "Merlyn Stone" and by 2006 "underground beta versions" of the

Book of Elven-Faerie started "mysteriously" showing up on the internet.

In 2008, a modern revival movement toward uncovering the truths of Sumerians, Babylonians (and Egyptians) and the Anunnaki appeared in public under the umbrella of "Mardukite Ministries."

ENOCHIAN THEORY

Enochian magick was allegedly given to mankind by "angels" via two men in the late 1500's. John Dee and Edward Kelley kept vast records of many communications with the "angels", which has been called in modern times both "the magick of the *Necronomicon*" and also the "most powerful system of Western Magick".

Whether we are to take the system at face value as a mystical tradition derived from Gnostic-Christian based magick or that it lends an eye to something much deeper into the forgotten gods of the Middle East (called the *Anunnaki*), it is not certain – but the revival of the magick in the New Age has certainly not overlooked the evocative nature of being able to commune directly with these forces.

ENOCHIAN ALPHABET

The "angelic alphabet" used in Enochian Magick as divined by John Dee and Edward Kelley. It is used in the construction of the Enochian Tablets so that the spirits being conjured will better recognize them. The alphabet has two forms: a deliberate "ceremonial" form and a cursive form used in more expeditious writing. Other "celestial alphabets" also appear infrequently in the New Age, but none carry the same tradition of historical use like the Enochian alphabet.

	Ceremonial	Cursive			Ceremonial	Cursive
B (pe)				P (mals)		
C,K (veh)				Q (ger)		
G (ged)				N (drun)		
D (gal)				X (pal)		
F (orth)				O (med)		
A (un)				R (don)		
E (graph)				Z (ceph)		
M (tal)				W,U,V (Vau)		
I,J,Y (gan)				S (fam)		
H (nahath)				T (gisa)		
L (ur)						

150

JOHN DEE & EDWARD KELLEY

Fascinated with astrology, John Dee publicly prophesized the time that Queen Mary would die and it came to pass. He was accused of using black magick to kill her and eventually imprisoned. When her sister, Queen Elizabeth I ascended the throne proper, she released Dee and made him her personal royal court astrologer. In spite of his position, financial stress forced Dee to continue his alchemical pursuits for the philosopher's stone. This interest led him to the company of a young rogue-seer named Edward Kelley. As little as we know truly of Dee's life, we know even less about his partner Kelley, except that they spent many years together allegedly conversing with angelic spirits, which led to the birth of the Enochian System.

John Dee excelled at ceremonial magick, so he would act as the magician while Kelley skryed into a crystal ball to decipher messages and letters of the Enochian Alphabet. A very complex ritual system was created or channeled (depending on your opinion) including the construction of the *Sigillum Dei Aemeth* and the Enochian Tablets, all of which are used to summon the power of angelic spirits, or conjure them to physical appearance. John Dee was well acquainted with Divine Names, the Gnostic tradition and the Kabbalah, all of which is apparent in the Enochian System.

The relationship between Dee and Kelley started to turn when Kelley informed him that a spirit named Madimi instructed them to share their wives. While it is said that Dee eventually gave into Kelley, no one knows what really transpired except that the unique magickal partnership ended abruptly. This background and Kelley's reputation for mystical hoaxes has led many scholars to question the validity of the Enochian System. The credibility of the system is probably derived more from John Dee's contributions than Kelley's. Dee wrote many other unrelated treatises on ceremonial magick, including the *Hieroglyphic Monad*, before he died. The Enochian System appears to have been successfully employed in relatively recent years by both the Hermetic Order of the Golden Dawn (GD), who revived its contemporary use, as well as Aleister Crowley.

ENOCHIAN BASICS

It would seem from the records left behind that

neither John Dee or Edward Kelley were actually granted permission to use the system, meaning that they must have been using some other means of ceremonial magick to conduct the initial workings. Dee and Kelley worked together from 1582 to 1589. For a long time after their death, the *enochian manuscripts* were kept in a secret compartment within Dee's library. After that time, the Golden Dawn took possession of the material.

Judith Spencer, in her book *Satan's High Priest*, describes the use of enochian and planetary spirits in Satanic covens. The "black pope" of Satanism, Anton LaVey, even used his own version of the enochian keys based on the works of Aleister Crowley.

Enochian magick is dependent on the proper utterance of magickal or "divine" names – the names are vibrated or intoned syllable by syllable with the body and mind "emptied of all else" - the syllable is "inhaled" silently and then "exhaled" and intoned verbally.

The language of enochian magick is similar to hebrew or even older – Akkadian, Sumerian, etc. Each letter or two letters forms a syllable. Consonants are pronounced alone unless they are accompanied by a vowel. IBAH would then be spoken "ee-bah". MOR is pronounced "moh-ar". DMAL is "dee-mah-el" and BEIGIA is "beh-ee-gee-ah".

ENOCHIAN TABLETS

There are four "watchtower tablets" placed at their appropriate directions inside the magick circle and a re constructed based on Dee's writings from 12 inch by 13 inch square pieces of wood. There is also a smaller "Tablet of Union" kept on the central altar and two versions are shown of this in addition to the "Enochian Pentacle." Diagrams for what has just been described is given on the following pages.

```
r Z i l a f A y t l p a
a r d Z a i d p a l a m
c z o n s a r o Y a u b
T o i T t z o P a c o C
S i g a s o m r b z n h
f m o n d a T d i a r i
o r o i b a H a o z p i
t N a b r V i x g a s d
O i i i t T p a l o a i
A b a m o o o a C u c a
N a o c o T t n p r n T
o c a n m a g o t r o i
S h i a l r a p m Z o x
```

ENOCHIAN TABLET OF AIR

```
T a o A d u p t D n i m
a a b c o o r o m e b b
T o g c o n x m a l G m
n h o d D i a l e a o c
p a t A x i o V s P s N
S a a i x a a r V r o i
m p h a r s l g a i o l
M a m g l o i n L i r x
o l a a D n g a T a p a
p a L c o i d x P a c n
n d a z N z i V a a s a
i i d P o n s d A s p i
x r i n h t a r n d i L
```

ENOCHIAN TABLET OF WATER

ENOCHIAN TABLET OF EARTH

b	O	a	Z	a	R	o	p	h	a	R	a
u	N	n	a	x	o	P	S	o	m	d	n
a	i	g	r	a	n	o	o	m	a	g	g
o	r	p	m	n	i	n	g	b	e	a	i
r	S	O	n	i	z	i	r	l	e	m	u
i	z	i	n	r	C	z	i	a	M	h	l
M	O	r	d	i	a	l	h	C	t	G	a
O	C	a	n	c	h	i	a	s	o	m	t
A	r	b	i	z	m	i	i	l	p	i	z
O	p	a	n	a	L	a	m	s	m	a	p
d	O	l	o	p	i	n	i	a	n	b	a
r	x	p	a	o	c	s	i	z	i	x	p
a	x	t	i	r	V	a	s	t	r	i	m

ENOCHIAN TABLET OF FIRE

d	o	n	p	a	T	d	a	n	V	a	a
o	l	o	a	G	e	o	o	b	a	u	a
O	P	a	m	n	o	V	G	m	a	n	m
a	p	l	s	T	e	d	e	c	a	o	p
s	c	m	i	o	o	n	A	m	l	o	x
V	a	r	S	G	d	l	b	r	i	a	p
o	l	P	t	e	a	a	p	D	o	c	e
p	s	u	a	c	n	r	Z	i	r	Z	a
S	i	o	d	a	o	i	n	R	z	f	m
d	a	l	t	T	d	n	a	d	i	r	e
d	i	x	o	m	o	n	s	i	o	s	p
O	o	D	p	z	i	A	p	a	n	l	i
r	g	o	a	n	n	P	A	c	r	a	r

ENOCHIAN TABLET OF UNION
[ENOCHIAN]

E	X	A	R	P
H	C	O	M	A
N	A	N	T	A
B	I	T	O	M

TABLET OF UNION
[ENGLISH]

ENOCHIAN PENTACLE

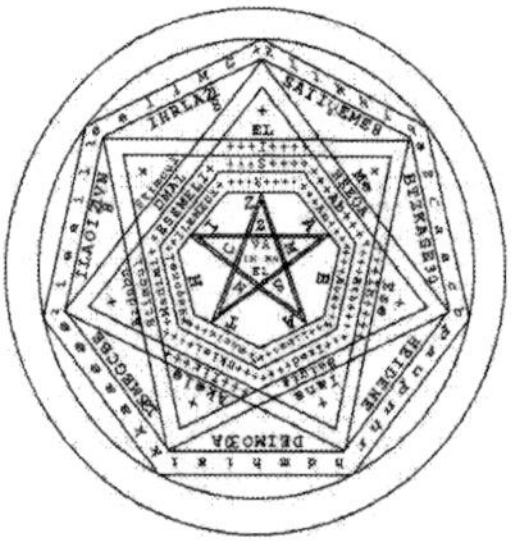

ENOCHIAN MAGICK

PREREQUISITE KNOWLEDGE

1. The name of the senior or angel to be evoked.
2. The direction/Watchtower to face, using elemental correspondences.
3. The Enochian Keys to be recited.
4. The hierarchy or order of succession to be called. Use this order:
    a) Divine Name of the element,
    b) King
    c) Seniors
    d) Cross-Angel: six lettered
    e) Cross-Angel: five lettered
5. The planetary-hexagram to be traced and the color to envision it.

HINTS & TIPS

1. Except for Kings, the hierarchy needs only to be followed until you reach the desired name.
2. A hexagram is traced only when you are evoking a Senior. All six must

be used to contact a King.

3. Use an "invoking pentagram" if evoking Cross-Angels.

4. If evoking a Cross-Angel, you need only speak the names of the Seniors, though some operators prefer to trace all corresponding hexagrams.

5. Hexagrams are ruled by planetary forces, while the pentagrams are ruled by the elements.

ORDER OF OPERATIONS

1. Enter the body of light and perform the Watchtower Ceremony.

2. Go to the appropriate direction/ Watchtower and trace the hexagram(s) or pentagram envisioning it a color correspondent to the planet or element.

3. Intone the descending Enochian hierarchy from the designated element. When calling the Kings, you must intone each name of the Senior while synchronously tracing the appropriate hexagrams.

4. Repeat the name of the entity many times. Envision it filling you and projecting from you. The spirit will appear in the traced star or some desired skrying speculum.
5. Perform the Lesser Banishing Ritual of the Pentagram (LBRP) when finishing the rite.

DIVINE NAMES – WATCHTOWERS

Air: Oro Ibah Aozpi
(*oh-roh ee-bah ah-oh-zod-pee*)
Water: Mph Arsl Gaiol
(*em-peh-heh ar-ess-el gah-ee-oh-leh*)
Earth: Mor Dial Hktga
(*moh-ar dee-al-el heh-keh-teh-gah*)
Fire: Oip Teaa Pdoke
(*oh-ee-peh teh-ah-ah peh-doh-key*)

ENOCHIAN ELEMENTAL KINGS

Air: Bataivah (*bah-tah-ee-vah-heh*)
Water: Raagiosl (*rah-ah-gee-ohs-el*)
Earth: Ikzhikal (*ee-keh-zod-he-kah-el*)
Fire: Edlprnaa (*ee-del-por-nah-ah*)

ENOCHIAN PLANETARY SENIORS

[*Order listed*: Mars, Jupiter, Moon,
Venus, Mercury, Sun.]
Air: Habioro, Aaozaif, Htmorda,
Ahaozpi, Avtotar, Hipotga
Water: Srahpm, Saiinou, Laoaxrp,
Slgaiol, Soniznt, Ligdisa
Earth: Laidrom, Akzinor, Lzinopo,
Alhktga, Ahmllvk, Likiansa
Fire: Aaetpio, Adaeoet, Alnkdood,
Aapdoke, Anadoin, Arinnap

ENOCHIAN KEYS
FOR KINGS & SENIORS

Air: 1, 2 and 3
Water: 1, 2 and 4
Earth: 1, 2 and 5
Fire: 1, 2 and 6

ENOCHIAN KEYS
FOR SUBORDINATE
CROSS-ANGELS

Air of Air: Idoigo, Aroza (3)
Water of Air: Lkalza, Palam (3 & 7)

Earth of Air: Aaioao, Oiiit (3 & 8)
Fire of Air: Aovrrs, Aloai (3 & 9)
Air of Water: Obgota, Abako (4 & 10)
Water of Water: Nelapr, Omebb (4)
Earth of Water: Maladi, Olaad (4 & 11)
Fire of Water: Iaaasd, Atapi (4 & 12)
Air of Earth: Angpol, Vnnax (5 & 13)
Water of Earth: Anaeem, Sonda (5 & 14)
Earth of Earth: Abalpt, Arbiz (5)
Fire of Earth: Ompnir, Ilpiz (5 & 15)
Air of Fire: Noalmr, Oloag (6 & 16)
Water of Fire: Vadali, Obava (6 & 17)
Earth of Fire: Volxdo, Sioda (6 & 18)
Fire of Fire: Rzionr, Nrzfn (6)

MOON

MERCURY

VENUS

SUN

MARS

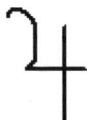

JUPITER

SATURN

HEXAGRAMS

Hexagrams are commonly found in ceremonial and high magick. Though the figure corresponds to the number six, "high ceremonialists" use it to show the forces of the seven alchemical and ancient planets, six rays with the Sun at the center.

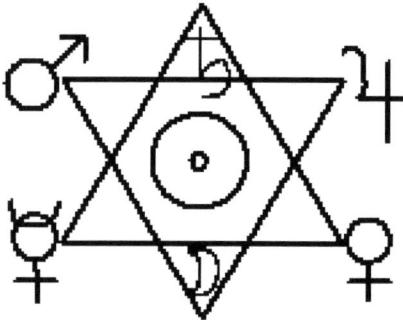

In some traditions, the top point represents the **Sun** and the bottom represents the Moon, meanwhile the four elements (air, earth, fire & water) exist in between. In Hermetic interpretations, the hexagram represents the energetic exchange between "above" and "below" with the Higher Self, whereas the pentagram is drawing up the power of the elements from the Earth Planet. The Hexagram is also sacred to the Hebrew tradition and the Kabbalah.

Hexangle of the Elements

Invoking Hexagram of Saturn

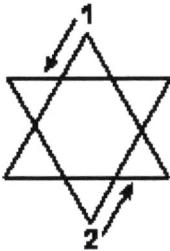

Banishing Hexagram of
Saturn

Invoking Hexagram of Moon

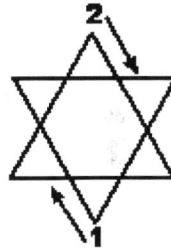

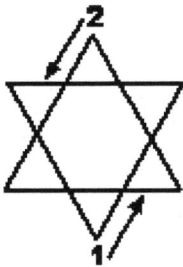

Banishing Hexagram of
Moon

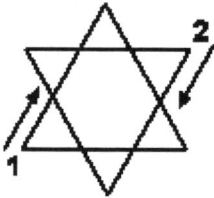

Invoking Hexagram of
Mercury

Banishing Hexagram of
Mercury

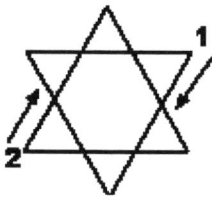

Invoking Hexagram of
Jupiter

Banishing Hexagram of Jupiter

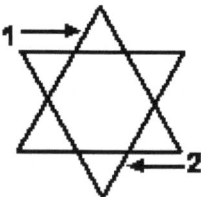

Invoking Hexagram of Mars

Banishing Hexagram of Mars

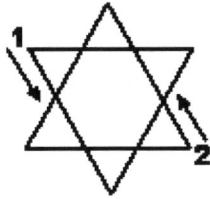

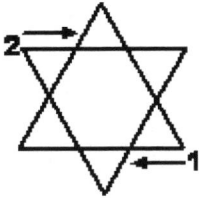

Invoking Hexagram of Venus

Banishing Hexagram of Venus

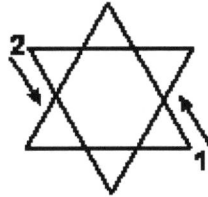

Invoking Hexagram of Saturn
(Thelemic)

Banishing Hexagram of Saturn
(Thelemic)

ENOCHIAN KEYS (CALLS)

THE FIRST ENOCHIAN KEY

I reign over you says the God of Justice, in power exalted above the firmaments of Wrath. In whose hands the Sun is as a sword and the Moon as a through-thrusting fire: Who measures your garments in the midst of my ventures and trussed you together as the palms of my hands: Whose seats I garnished with the Fire of Gathering: Who beautified your garments with admiration: To whom I made a law to govern the Holy Ones: Who delivered you with a rod and with the Ark of Knowledge. Moreover you lifted up your voices and swore obedience and faith to Him that lives and triumphs: Whose beginning is not nor can ever be: Which shines as a flame in the midst of your palaces and reigns among you as a balance of righteousness and truth. Move, therefore and show yourselves: open the mysteries of your creation. Be friendly unto me. For I am the servant of the same, your God, the true worshiper of the Highest.

THE SECOND ENOCHIAN KEY

Can the Wings of Wind understand your voices of wonder, O you the Second of the First, whom the burning flames have formed within the depths of my jaws: Whom I have prepared as cups for a wedding or the flowers in their beauty for the chamber of righteousness. Stronger are your feet than the barren stone and mightier are your voices than the manifold winds. For you are becoming a building that is not, except in the mind of the All-Powerful. Arise, says the First. Move, therefore unto thy servants. Show yourselves in power and make me a strong seer of things, for I am descended from Him that lives forever.

THE THIRD ENOCHIAN KEY

Behold, says your God. I am a circle on whose hands stand Twelve Kingdoms. Six are the seats of the living breath, the rest are sharp sickles or the horns of death, wherein the creatures of Earth are and are not, except by my own hands that also sleep and shall rise. In the First, I made you stewards and placed you on Twelve Seats of Government, giving unto every one of you the power over Four, Five and Six, the true ages of time: to the intent that the highest vessels and the corners of your government you shall work my power: pouring down the Fires of Life and increase continually upon the Earth. Thus you have become the skirts of justice and truth. In the names of the same, your God, lift up, I say to you. Behold, his mercies flourish and his name becomes mighty against us, as unto the initiates of the Secret Wisdom of your creation.

THE FOURTH ENOCHIAN KEY

I have set my feet in the South and have looked about me saying: Are not the thunders of increase numbered 33, which reign in the Second Angle? Under whom I have placed 9.639 whom none have numbered but One: In whom the Second beginning of things are and wax strong, which successively are the numbers of Time, and their powers are the First. Arise you Sons of Pleasure and visit the Earth: For I am the Lord your God which is and lives forever. In the name of the Creator, move and show yourselves as pleasant deliverers so that you may praise Him among the Sons of Men.

171

THE FIFTH ENOCHIAN KEY

The mighty sounds have entered the Third Angle and become as olives on the olive mount, looking with gladness upon the Earth and dwelling in the brightness of the heavens as continual comforters. Unto whom I have fastened 19 pillars of gladness and gave them vessels to water the Earth with all of her creatures: And they are the brothers of the First and Second, and the beginning of the own seats which are garnished with 69,636 continually burning lamps, whose numbers are as the First, the End, and the midway content of time. Therefore come and obey your creation. Visit us in peace and comfort. Include us the receivers of your mysteries. For why? Our Lord and Master is of the All-One.

THE SIXTH ENOCHIAN KEY

The spirits of the Fourth Angle are nine, mighty in the firmaments of water: the First has planted a torment to the wicked and a garland to the righteous: Giving unto them fiery darts to wash the Earth, and 7,699 continual workmen whose courses visit with comfort to the Earth, and are in government and continuance as the Second and the Third. Wherefore, come and follow my voice. I have talked of you and I move you in power and presence: Whose works shall be a song of honor and the praise of your God in your creation.

THE SEVENTH ENOCHIAN KEY

The East is a house of virgins singing praises among the flames of the First glory, wherein the Lord has opened his mouth and they become 28 living dwellings in whom the strength of man rejoices and are appareled with ornaments of brightness, such a work that fascinates all creatures: Whose kingdoms and continuance are as the Third and Fourth, strong towers and places of comfort, the seat of mercy and continuance. O you servants of mercy, move, appear, and sing praises unto the Creator of All. And be might among us. For to this covenant is given power and our strength waxes strong in our comforter.

THE EIGHTH ENOCHIAN KEY

The midday, the First, is as the Third Heaven made of 26 crystalline pillars, in whom the elders are becoming strong, which I have prepared for my own righteousness, says the Lord: Whose long continuance shall be as buckles to the Stooping Dragon and like unto the harvest of a widow. How many are there which remain in the glory of the Earth, which are, and shall not see death until this house falls and the Dragon sinks? Come away for the thousands have spoken! Come away for the Crown of the Temple and the robe of Him that is, was and shall be crowned King and divided. Come! Appear unto the terror of the Earth and unto our com-fort and to those who are prepared.

THE NINTH ENOCHIAN KEY

A mighty guard of Fire with two-edged swords flaming, which have eight Vials of Wrath for Two times and a half, whose wings are wormwood and of the marrow of salt, have settled their feet in the West and are measured by their 9,996 ministers. These gather up the moss of the Earth as the rich man does guard his treasure. Cursed are they whose iniquities they are. In their eyes are millstones greater than the Earth and from their mouth runs seas of blood. Their heads are covered with diamonds and upon their hands are marble sleeves. Happy is he on whom they frown not. For why? The God of Righteousness rejoices in them. Come away and not your Vials, for the time is such that requires comfort.

THE TENTH ENOCHIAN KEY

The thunders of judgment and wrath are num-bered and are harbored in the North in the likeness of an Oak whose branches are 22 nests of lamentation and weeping laid up for the Earth, which burns night and day: And vomit out the heads of scorpions and active sulfur mingled with poison. These are the thunders that 5678 times (in the 24th part of your moment) roar with a hundred might earthquakes and a thousand times as many surges, which rest not, neither know any echoing time herein. One rock brings forth a thousand, as occurs in the hearts of men with their thoughts. Woe! Woe! Woe! Woe! Woe! Woe! Woe! Woe! Woe! Hear, I say, Woe! Be merciful to the Earth for her iniquity is, was and shall be great. Come away! But not your mighty sounds.

THE ELEVENTH ENOCHIAN KEY

The mighty seat groaned aloud and there were five thunders, which flew into the East and the Eagle spoke and cried in a loud voice: Come away! And they gather-ed themselves together and became the House of Death, of whom it is measured, and it is 31. Come away! For I have prepared for you a place. Move therefore and show yourselves. Open the mysteries of your creation. Be friendly unto me, for I am a servant of the same, your God, who is the true worshiper of the Highest.

THE THIRTEENTH ENOCHIAN KEY

O you swords of the South, which have 42 eyes to stir up the wrath of Sin: making men drunken and empty. Behold, the promise of God and His power, which is called amongst you a bitter string. Move and show yourselves. Open the mysteries of your creation. Be friendly unto me, for I am a servant of the same, your God, who is the true worshiper of the Highest.

THE FOURTEENTH ENOCHIAN KEY

O you Sons of Fury, the legal heirs of the just, which sits upon 24 seats, vexing all creatures of the Earth with age, which have under them 1,636. Behold the Voice of God, the promise of Him, which is called amongst you Fury or extreme justice. Move, therefore and show yourselves. Open the mysteries of your creation. Be friendly unto me, for I am a servant of the same, your God, who is the true worshiper of the Highest.

THE FIFTEENTH ENOCHIAN KEY

O thou, the Governor of the First Flame under whose wings are 6,739, which weave the Earth with dryness: Which knows the secret of the Great Name: righteousness, and the Seal of Honor. Move, therefore and show yourselves. Open the mysteries of your creation. Be friendly unto me, for I am a servant of the same, your God, who is the true worshiper of the Highest.

THE SIXTEENTH ENOCHIAN KEY

O thou, Governor of the Second Flame, the

House of Justice, who has your beginning in glory and shall comfort the just, who walks the Earth with 8,763 feet, which understands and separates the creatures. Great you are to the God of Conquest. Move, therefore and show yourselves. Open the mysteries of your creation. Be friendly unto me, for I am a servant of the same, your God, who is the true worshipper of the Highest.

THE SEVENTEENTH ENOCHIAN KEY

O thou, Governor of the Third Flame who wings are the thorns to stir up vexation. And who has 7,336 living lamps going before thee: Whose God is wrath in anger, bind up thy loins and take notice! Move, therefore and show yourselves. Open the mysteries of your creation. Be friendly unto me, for I am a servant of the same, your God, who is the true worshiper of the Highest.

THE EIGHTEENTH ENOCHIAN KEY

O thou, the might light and burning flame of comfort, which opens the Glory of God unto the center of the Earth. I whom the 6,332 secrets of

Truth have their abiding, which is called in your kingdom of Joy and not to be measured. Be thou a window of comfort unto me. Move, therefore and show yourselves. Open the mysteries of your creation. Be friendly unto me, for I am a servant of the same, your God, who is the true worshiper of the Highest.

ADVANCED ENOCHIAN MAGICK

The fragmented spiritual dimensions from which the angelic spirits of the Enochian System are called. This lore is at the heart of one of the least employed of all operations of high magick in the New Age, "Rising on the Planes." This covert work is quite advanced, executed in its entirety from the "Body of Light" and typically conducted by only the most adept operators of ceremonial magick. It is a lengthy process to work through all thirty of the aethyrs successfully, requiring a strong feat of concentration using skrying or "spirit vision" while simultaneously conducting ritual gestures and incantations (although this can just as successfully be conducted on the astral plane).

In the formulation of the system, John Dee, the ritual magician, required the aid of a seer or co-magician (Edward Kelley). Rising on the Planes requires the passage through or attainment of the first eighteen Enochian Keys before executing the first of thirty cycles of the Call to the Aethyrs. This "call" is the same for all of the aethyrs except that the title of each plane is re-

placed. Appropriate sigils of the angelic guard-
ians/governors of each aethyr should be carried
as seals, traced and envisioned in the air while
calling the appropriate Divine Name for each
spirit. Each aethyr is also aligned to a fundamental element, which determines the ritual dir-

ection to face and the magickal weapon used to trace the sigils.

Each of the aethyrs must be accessed consecutively. though some confusion occurs here since half of the traditions work from the thirtieth to

16 LEA	a)	b)	c)
17 TAN	a)	b)	c)
18 ZEN	a)	b)	c)
19 POP	a)	b)	c)
20 KHR	a)	b)	c)
21 ASP	a)	b)	c)
22 LIN	a)	b)	c)
23 TOR	a)	b)	c)
24 NIA	a)	b)	c)
25 VTI	a)	b)	c)
26 DES	a)	b)	c)
27 ZAA	a)	b)	c)
28 BAG	a)	b)	c)
29 RII	a)	b)	c)
30 TEX	a)	b)	c)	d)

the first and the other half follow the opposite regimen. Once an individual relationship has been established between the wizard and the guardian spirits of the first eighteen Enochian Keys, the operation of the Call to the Aethyrs will be sufficient to access these planes via astral " spirit vision." The names and sigils of the aethyrs are derived from the Enochian Tablets.

A phonetic key is provided for the title of each aethyr, derived from the keys provided by the Golden Dawn System, though there is some debate over their accuracy.

1. LIL (*lee-lah*) [water] Occodon, Pascomb, Valgars
2. ARN (*ah-rah-noo*) [water] Doagnis, Pacasna, Dialiva
3. ZOM (*zoad-oh-me*) [water] Samapha, Virooli, Andispi
4. PAZ (*pah-zoad*) [water] Thotanf, Axziarg, Pothnir
5. LIT (*lee-tay*) [water] Lazdixi, Nocamal, Tiarpax
6. MAZ (*mah-zoad*) [fire] Saxtomp, Vavaamp, Zirzird
7. DEO (*day-oh*) [fire] Obmacas, Genadol, Aspiaon

8. ZID (*zoad-ee-dah*) [fire] Zamfres, Todnaon, Pristac

9. ZIP (*zoad-ee-pay*) [fire] Oddiorg, Cralpir, Doanzin

10. ZAX (*zoad-ahtz*) [union] Lexarph, Comanan, Tabitom

11. ICH (*ee-kah-hey*) [water] Molpand, Vanarda, Ponodol

12. LOE (*loh-aye*) [fire] Tapamal, Gedoons, Ambrial

13. ZIM (*zoad-ee-me*) [fire] Gecaond, Laparin, Docepax

14. VTA (*vah-tah*) [air] Tedoond, Vivipos, Ooanamb

15. OXO (*ohx-oh*) [air] Tehando, Nociabi, Tastoxo

16. LEA (*lah-ay-ah*) [air] Cocarpt, Lanaconi, Sochial

17. TAN (*tah-noo*) [air] Sigmorf, Aydropt, Tocarzi

18. ZEN (*zoad-en*) [air] Nabaomi, Zafasai, Yalpamb

19. POP (*poh-pay*) [air] Torzoxi, Abaiond, Omagrap

20. KHR (*kay-hay-ray*) [air] Zildron, Parziba, Totocan

21. ASP (*ah-ess-pay*) [air] Chirspa, Toantom, Vixpalg

22. LIN (*lee-noo*) [air] Oxidaia, Paraoan,

Calzirg

23. TOR (*toh-ray*) [earth] Ronoamb, Onizimp, Zaxanin
24. NIA (*nee-ah*) [earth] Orcamir, Chialps, Soageel
25. VTI (*vah-tee*) [earth] Mirzind, Obvaors, Ranglam
26. DES (*day-ess*) [earth] Pophand, Nigrana, Bazchim
27. ZAA (*zoad-ah-ah*) [earth] Saziama, Mathula, Korpamb
28. BAG (*bah-gee*) [earth] Labnixp, Focisni, Oxlopar
29. RII (*ree-ee*) [earth] Vastrim, Odraxti, Gomziam
30. TEX (*tehtz*) [water] Taoagla, Gemnimb, Advorpt, Dozinal

CALL OF THE AETHYRS

Also known as "Rising on the Planes," this advanced operation of ceremonial magick is derived from the Enochian Tradition and used as part of the Golden Dawn System (GD). This operation is partially physic-ally ritualized and partly astral in nature, using "spirit vision" to visit the aethyr dimensions. Beginners must evoke the *18 Enochian Keys* before calling the

30 aethyrs. The planes should be risen on individually. When sufficient experience is gained, the wizard may not need to work through subordinate gates each time.

1. Perform the Watchtower Ceremony.
2. Face the appropriate direction based on the elemental correspondence of the aethyr.
3. Enter the body of light.
4. Recite the "Call of the Aethyr" inserting the appropriate name of the aethyr.
5. Evoke the Angelic Guardians (governors) of the aethyr while tracing their sigils in the air visualizing them in an appropriate color (element based).
6. Leave the body using skrying or astral projection, allowing the astral body (or mental projection) to rise freely on that plane/aethyr.
7. Retrace the sigils in reverse to dismiss the spirits and perform the Lesser Banishing Ritual of the Pentagram (LBRP) to complete the rite, negating any residual energies of the nemeton.

The "Call of the Aethyr" is referred to as the 19th through 48th Enochian Keys, depending on the name of the aethyr inserted. The version provided immediately below has been translated to English, and is especially recommended for beginners to this form of magick. The wizard should never intone incomprehensible words and formulas until the symbolism of such can be understood. The same applies to Divine Names. After becoming more proficient with the Enochian System and language, you can use the "Enochian version."

Key to the Aethyrs
(English)

The heavens that dwell in the *N.* aethyr are mighty in the parts of the Earth and execute the judgment of the Highest. Unto you it is said: Behold the face of your God, the beginning of comfort, whose eyes are the brightest in the heavens, which provided you for the govern-ment of Earth and her unspeakable variety, furnishing you with a powerful understanding to dispose all things according to the providence of him that sits at the Holy Throne and rose up in the beginning saying: The Earth, let her be governed by her parts and let there be division in her that the glory of her may be always drunken and vexed in itself. Her course, let it circulate with the heavens and as a handmaiden let her serve them. One season, let it confound another, and let there be no creature upon or with her one and the same. All her members let them differ in their qualities and let there be no one creature equal to another. The reasonable creature of Earth, and men, let them vex and weed out one another and their dwelling places. Let them forget their names. The work of man and his pompousness; let them be defaced. His buildings; let them become caves for the beasts of the field. Confound her under-standing with darkness. For why? I repent that I have made man. One moment, let her be known, in another moment, a stranger. Because she is the bed of a harlot and the dwelling place of him that is Fallen. O ye heavens arise! The lower heavens beneath you; let them serve you! Govern those that govern. Cast down such as fall. Bring forth those who increase and destroy the rotten. Let no place remain in one number. Add and diminish until the stars are numbered. Arise! Move! And appear before the covenant of his mouth, which he has sworn to us in his justice. Open the mysteries of your creation and make us partakers of the undefiled knowledge.

Key to the Aethyrs
(Enochian)

Madriaax d s praf *N*. aethyr chis micaolz saanir od fisis bal zizras Iaida. Nonca gohulim: micma adoian mad, Iaod bliorb, soba ooaona chis Lucifitias Piripsol, ds abraassa nonif net aaib caosgi od tilb adphant damploz, tooatnoncfg Miadz Oma Irasd tol glo marb Yarry Id oigo od torxup Iaodaf gohol: Ca osga tabaord saanir od Christeos yrpoil tiobl busdir tilb noaln paid orsba od dodrmni zylna. Elzap tilb parm gi piripsax, od ta qurist booapis L hibm ovcho symp od Christeos ag toltorn mirc q tiobl L el. Tol paomd dilzmo as pian od Christeos ag L toltorn parach asymp. Cordziz, dodpal od didalz L smnad: of fargt bams omaoas. Conishra od avavox, tonug Orsca tbl noasmi tabges levithmong. Un chi omp tibl ors. Bagle? Modoah ol cordziz. L capimao izomax-ip, od cacocasb gosaa. Baglem pi tianta a babalond, od foorgt teloc vovim. Madriax torzu! Oadviax orocho aboapri! Tabaori priaz artabas. Adrpan cors ta dobix. Lolcam priazi ar coazior, of Quasb Qting. Ripir paoxt sala cor. Vml od prdzar carcg aoiveae cormpt. Torzu. Zacar. Od zamran aspt sibsi butmona, ds surza tiaballa Odo cicle qaa, od ozozma plapli Iadnamad.

AZRAEL & CONJURATIONS

The magickal ability to conjure or evoke spiritual entities to physical appearance is one of the most advanced uses of ceremonial magick conducted by Adept Wizards. Fortunately, wizards are able to call on the powers extended by entities without causing these spirits to expend the energy necessary to transition and make a physical apparition. Many masters consider the forcing of a spiritual manifestation of this sort to be especially unwise. It is better to use a black mirror or other skrying medium to meet the spirit on the Astral Plane using "spirit vision." Doing so will ensure the safety of the mage and conserve the energy necessary to accomplish a task, which is not the summ-oning of the spirit itself, but the use of their metaphysical abilities. It is therefore not advised to focus energy on the physical manifestation of the spirit, but instead concentrate on connecting with the energy current requested from the entity.

The relationship between wizards and the hierarchies of spirits and angels they command is historically a stressed one. Any simple analysis of the classical grimoires will reveal this. Magicians make demands of spirits harshly, sometimes threatening them and even cursing them by the Divine Names if they do not readily appear. These same mages would spend an unending amount of energy trying to protect them from the same energies they were calling by force. A rational and ethical wizard will find such a relationship absurd and counterproductive to the Great Work. If after three request and thirty minutes has passed without results, do not despair, but end the rite. Close out with the Lesser Banishing Ritual of the Pentagram (LBRP) and dismiss the spirit as though it did arrive (in case there is any residual energy) and make notes of the conditions and your experience. You may or may not decide to try the same rite again under different conditions (seasons, lunar phases, etc.).

Mystics are aware of the universal oneness that is all of seen and unseen existence. They understand the spirit world in a somewhat different way than the wizard. The spirits being commanded are in actuality a part of ourselves, and it is the fragmentation or individualization of our existence that causes us to perceive these other beings as being separate. The wizard must observe the same laws, but the ritualized effort is different. The separation and then union with the essence of spiritual beings is performed with the use of a magick mirror, often constructed from Solomon's Triangle as a skrying device for spiritual evocation.

When the Hermetic Order of the Golden Dawn (GD) performed evocations, they did so in the most elaborately cast circles. The Enochian and Elemental Tablets are used, along with the Tablet of Union. The LBRP, Watchtower Ceremony and Supreme Invoking Ritual of the Pentagram (SIRP) are used in succession as opening rites. Pentagrams and hexagrams are traced in appropriate quarters depending on the nature of the spirit being evoked (while simultaneously calling out for them.) In some instances, the grimoires suggest that you work through a "pantheon" or "hierarchy" of spiritual entities in order to summon the powers of the specific spirit.

193

In high magick and the Enochian System, the Divine Names and Holy Names of angels are held in such high regard that the proper utterance of the name alone in ritual is sufficient to signal that entity's attention. All Holy Names are usually called in out in a series of syllables, based on the phonetic language they are based on. The act of writing phonetically (using sound rather than adherence to grammar) extends back to the ancient Sumerian Tradition. The operator clears their mind and then focuses on each utterance (syllable) and its significance. Summon the energy around you and inhale, using meditative breathing.

While exhaling the tone, feel the energy radiate out from the *nemeton*. Some have suggested that the characters of the names themselves should be visualized in either Enochian or Hebrew, depending on the traditions being observed. In the *Keys of Solomon*, the operator follows a basic formula of first praying to the Source of All, invoking the Tetragrammaton and the (Gnostic-Hermetic) Divine Names, and then speaking a conjuration specifically toward the entity.

Hundreds of different prayers and conjurations can be accumulated from the various grimoires.

However, Abraham the Jew, the scion of the *Sacred Book of Magick of Abramelin the Mage*, recommends that wizards write their own prayers from the heart. In many instances, the conjurations found in classical grimoires can be in excess of a dozen paragraphs long. The kabbalistic one included here is derived from the more successfully used versions (according to the notebooks kept by the *Elven Fellowship Circle of Magick*).

THE GREAT CONJURATION OF SOLOMON
(Edited from Book I:V, *Keys of Solomon*)

I conjure ye spirit *N.* by the power, virtue and wisdom of the spirit and the Name of God, by the undefiled knowledge, by the mercy, strength, greatness and unification of God; and by the Divine Name EHEIEH, in which all other Holy Names derive their existence. I conjure ye spirit *N.* by YOD, the name representing the simplicity and Divine Unification of God and all Creation. I conjure ye spirit *N.* by the Tetragrammaton: YOD-HEH-VAHV-HEH EL-OHIM, which expresses the might and majesty of God and all of creation. I conjure ye spirit *N.* by the strength and mercy of EL. I conjure ye spirit *N.* by the omnipotent name ELOHIM GIBOR. I conjure ye spirit *N.* by the Divine Name, ELOAH VA-DAATH, the God of Israel. I conjure ye spirit *N.* by ELOHIM TZABA-OTH, the God revealed in undefiled knowledge. I conjure ye spirit *N.* by the name EL ADONAI TZABAOTH, the God of armies. I conjure ye spirit *N.* by SHADDAI EL CHYE, the Divine Name of the Living God. Finally I conjure ye spirit *N.* by ADO-NAI MELEKH, the name invoked by Joshua. Yes, spirit *N.* I conjure you here by all of the Holy Names of God. Move now from your darkness and show yourself by the power of the Source of All Being and Creation.

AZRAEL & DEATH

In our present-day society we have come to perceive death from a purely religious per-spective, and thus our attitudes towards it is reflected from what we have been conditioned to believe. This generally comes in two flavors: firstly, one might fear death because it is the end of all things and an invitation into non-existence, or secondly, one might invite death because it is the means to an end and an invitation into some "heavenly" abode. As the

196

wise one's have said: "What is there to fear in death?" and "When was I ever *less* by dying?"

While the concept of death is easily glorified negatively or conjured into gruesome imagery, before one can ever hope to pragmatically work with "death energy," a clear understanding of what it truly is must be held in mind.

Death is a beautiful twilight euphoria of a "threshold" or "between" state that occurs when the consciousness leaves one physical incarnation or simulacrum for another. Death, therefore becomes the "vehicle" by which this occurs, and perhaps there is no more "occult" or "magickal" concept then death. It is the ancestors who we honor at Samhain (Halloween) and the intelligent spirits of the "between" that are contacted in grimoires.

By some esoteric definitions, "death" is the pure absence of life in physical matter. But it is said that matter cannot exist in the light without being inhabited by some spirit of light, so there is obviously another part of that yin-yang in the spirit world and that is death.

The spirit of light and death make life. And so those who work in the ways of *"Westgate Nec-*

romantics" have a kinship or magnetic resonance with this current, a means of getting "back in touch" with the "death energy." These practices *do not* condone necrophilia or desecration in any way. Working with this energy current through necromantics is different than "necromancy," which is the art of diving information from dead spirits or conjuring them to physical appearance using the instructions from medieval-styled grimoires.

The foremost leaders in these practices, including those who maintained the Westgate Death Museum in New Orleans (Leilah Wendell), suggest direct contact with death in order to align with it. While many people are looked at as simply "crazy" for their fixations on such, there are certainly going to be some readers who *just know* exactly what I am talking about, and curiously, the role of the "occult" seems to always come into play, and for good reason.

Cultures in the past had an increased appreciation for death, ancestors, bloodlines and caretaking (for elders), as well as extraordinary rites and incantations to be said over a person who is dying or recently has died, especially evident in various "*Books of the Dead.*" It is therefore not uncommon to find "death energy magicians"

198

working in mortuaries and spending time at funerals and cemeteries.

A true self-initiation into the role of death magic is to undertake a "death watch," which requires spending a night alone within an "inhabited" crypt or mausoleum. And it should be understood that these instructions are based only on the reports of what others have done and have nothing to do with what is necessarily condoned by the current author, especially in light of civil laws regarding such properties. While the practices of the Babylonian and Egyptian oriented *Necronomicon* are heavily dependent on the use of *lapis lazuli* stones during ritual, the amethyst appears particularly often in Leilah Wendell's Westgate necromantics, in addition is the recommendation of the use of jasmine incense.

APPEARING IN THE
DREAMS OF ANOTHER

An incredible mystic skill and used by many types of mystics – from sorcerer wizards to the alien illuminati, the ability to reach people in their sleep, particularly the active subconscious dream state. For the actual ritualization of this effort you will need an image of the person and preferably access to personal items of theirs or something that they have given to you.

This working is often used for one of two reasons, because to be sure, there are limited uses of dream access outside of emergency and mind control that do not either deal with: making love to a person in dreams or bringing nightmares.

The most often colors found in these Illuminati rites are red and black – an thus the Red Rite is often used to appear in forms that are acts of lust and the Black Rite is used to torment them. Use the color symbolism throughout the ritual setting. No specific verbiage is required but can be written to supplement the practitioner. Incense for the workings are required to achieve the proper mental sensations if this cannot be done artificially (*without physical means*). The Red Rite calls for jasmine and/or sandalwood and the Black Rite recommends myrrh or sandalwood. Dragon's blood is also popular. These forms of magick require the raising of intense emotional energy and incredible focus during its release. Sex Magick (usually in the form of masturbation) can also be used to aid in achieving these results.

THE NECRONOMICON

Many have purchased but few have actually read "the book," and yet many have come to believe that the magick and power to be gained from the *Necronomicon* is self-destructive, or worse, that by merely reading the book, you may go crazy or even die! Sorcerers and wizards of the modern age do not take the potential power of the *Necronomicon* lightly.

Not all mystical practitioners use it, or delve into it, but based on the attention its attracted in the contemporary "New Age," most of the learned mages seem to at least be aware of it. When I say, "the book," I specifically mean the infamous "Simon edition" mass-produced by the Avon House (now Harper-Collins) in the late 1970's. It remains the widest distributed occult text, carried by every mainstream bookseller and surviving over fifty printings!

The marketing and promotions of the book was extremely hyped up for the masses, including a strong notation on the back of the book stating that some people were not ready to cope with the psychological forces that the *Necronomicon* might expose its user to. Unfortunately, as a result of some of the hype with the Simon edition the *Necronomicon* has, for the most part, earned itself a "bad name." The Lovecraftian mythos that was originally the introduction to the idea for many, has not helped soothe this any. Due to the inherently dark overtones of the materials, it has even been believed to be a spellbook for devil-worship. And of course this could not be any farther from the truth (as a careful analysis of it would reveal), and the system evoked is no more or less "evil" than any other arcane occult system.

The notorious Simon edition of the *Necronomicon* is a "grimoire," conceptualized in the same tradition as the other supposed medieval texts which have been reprint-ed throughout the ages. And, like the others, it would appear to be a "notebook" only, not specifically a "training-manual" but a text written by one who was still learning and compiling a tradition that is alluded to be going extinct. And, just like the others, it would obviously appear to have things missing, almost as if being drawn from memory or written in haste. There is no preliminary primer in the practice of magick offered, partic-ularly concerning the Sumerian and Babylonian mythoi involved, so someone with no magickal foundations might have difficulty in simply opening it up and "using" it. Regardless, I would recommend obtaining a copy, should you take to this mythos.

While it may or may not be drawn from an actual collection titled: *Necronomicon*, the book does offer a practical application of researchable ancient magick, particularly the incantations that have been found on Chaldean, Akkadian and Babylonian tablets, such as those housed in the royal library of Ninevah. Some of these have been dated to second millennium BCE. So therefore, it is important to understand, forsaking Lovecraftian fantasies if necessarily, that the *Necronomicon* is at the very least a symbolic embodiment of a mythos and ancient current of power that is very real and alive.

BABYLONIAN MYTHOS

In the time before man, there was the first dragon, TIAMAT. TIAMAT ruled the Ancient Ones, a reptilian race of "evil" beings. They represent the "dragonmind," an unquenchable thirst for knowledge and power that is prevalent in the universe. Finally, TIAMAT gave birth to a son, MARDUK. MARDUK became the ruler of the Elder Gods, an oppositional army to the Ancient Ones.

MARDUK, empowered by the Solar God, ENKI, defeated his "evil" mother. Having cut the beast in half, he used half of her body to form the Heavens, and the other half to form the Earth. Empowered by ENKI, he fashioned a Gate to lock out the Ancient Ones from the time-space of mankind. It is known, in the *Necronomicon*, as the "Gate to the Outside." It cannot be opened except by one of the Sons of Man. The Seal of the Gate is known as the "Elder Sign."

It is written that MARDUK fashioned humans to keep watch over the Gate, so that the Ancient Ones would never come to rule again. He compiled a magickal lore for the Watchers of the Gate, and protections and exorcisms if the Ancient Ones were to seep out, or if their worshipers attempted to open the Gate. This magickal tradition came to be known as the *Necronomicon*.

NECRONOMICAL TABLETS

According to the Simon *Necronomicon*, the tradition evokes the powers of four elemental Gates, often represented with "tablets" comparable to that of the Enochian system. In fact, it has been believed that the "angelic" (*Anunnaki*) forces behind both the Enochian system and the Necronomicon have actually emerged from a singular ancient source. In the "About the Book" section of Gerald Schueler's Advanced Guide to Enochian Magick, the system is referred to as "that of the *Necronomicon*."

In the Enochian system, tablets are often used to decipher the sacred names to be incorporated within the ceremonial practices. Nearly all the tablets alluded to in the *Necronomicon* are indicative of "gates" or door-ways, a concept correlating well with the ancient Anun-naki concept of stargates. The colors used are always black and white, and when not indicated, doorways and gate symbols can be traced on the ground or on large pieces of poster-board or picture matting. Doing so aids the sorcerer in attracting the desired energy.

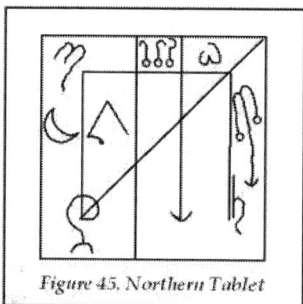
Figure 45. Northern Tablet

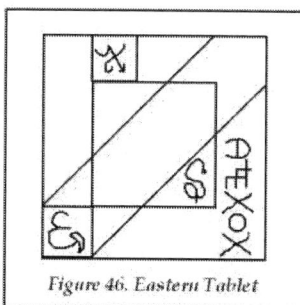
Figure 46. Eastern Tablet

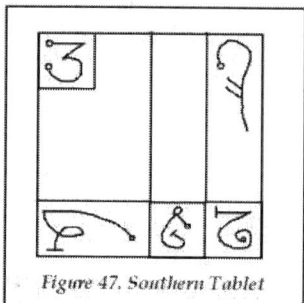
Figure 47. Southern Tablet

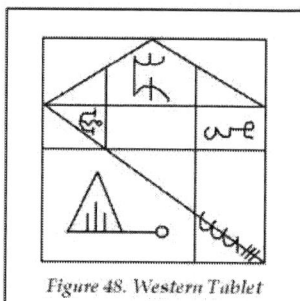
Figure 48. Western Tablet

Illustrations from "Arcanum" by Joshua Free

THE MAGICK CIRCLE
& PROTECTIONS

Descriptions of a specific manner in which to create a *nemeton* ("magick circle") is a common feature to the grimoires of old. Some of the

Kabbalistic-styled circles found in traditions of "high ceremonial magick" can actually become very elaborate operations. The more "shamanic" or "priestly" style of the *Necronomicon* offers a formula that is quite easy to utilize.

All the Necronomical workings are performed in circles made of flour, salt or chalk. This should be on a rock or dirt surface when performed outdoors. The circle should be nine feet in diameter and physically distinguishable. A little more than one foot from the markings, draw a smaller circle within the first one. Any watchtower tablets to be used should be placed in between the two circles at their appropriate directions.

The incense to be used should be that of pine, sandalwood, or cedar; you can use one or all of them, or two for that matter. When dealing with the "Watcher," the offering should be made of Oliberos, or nettles. The ritual circle is aligned to the north. On your altar or spreadcloth there should be two while pillar candles; the seal of the spirit or gate that you intend to be working with should be set between them. In the center of the circle, say:

ENU SHUB AM GIG ABSUKISH

EGIGGA GAR SHAG DA SISIE
AMARADA YA DINGIR UD KALAMA
SINIKU. DINGIR NINAG GUYU
NEXRRANIKU GA YA SHU
SHAGMUKU TU.

The incantation is believed to dispel undesired energies from the area, particularly malignant demons. The ancient culture that the *Necronomicon* is rooted in, held a strong belief and fear of demons. The Akkadians called them the "Maskim." Babylonian lore refers to the Queen of the Demons as LILITU or Lilith (and in Kabbalistic lore, Lilith is said to be the first wide of Adam in the Garden of Eden). Whatever it literally was, it would appear form the available lore that something mind-shatteringly dark was going on behind the scenes in these cultures.

It should be understood that the forces being dealt with in the *Necronomicon* require self-honesty and a pure spirit. Spiritual forces are on the Earth always and the magician is often given limited knowledge for protect-ion against such. In the current age, it is the Vatican under Catholicism that appears to hold the monopoly on sanctioning "exorcism" and yet a priest of the *Necronomicon* will have no difficulty in employing the protections against the Ancient Ones given in the Maklu Text. What is not so well-known, and is actually a secret kept by the Church today, is the powers held by the original "Lord's Prayer" and the "Prayer to St. Michael." Both are specifically applicable in this tradition. A careful examination of the Simon *Necronomicon* will actually reveal the suggestion of the use of the "Lord's Prayer" by the editor in his Introduction, stating:

> "Invocations using solar formulae have proven thus far effective in successfully banishing the demons and intelligences. For instance, the Kaddish prayer of the Jewish faith contains some solar elements that have proved resilient to inimical genii, and the vibration of the Lord's Prayer is also workable..."

VERSION ONE

Avvon d-bish-maiya, nith-qaddash shim-
    mukh. Tih-teh malchootukh.
Nih-weh çiw-yanukh: ei-chana d'bish-maiya:
    ap b'arah.
Haw lan lakh-ma d'soonqa-nan yoo-mana.
O'shwooq lan kho-bein: ei-chana d'ap kh'nan

209

shwiq-qan l'khayaween.

Oo'la te-ellan l'niss-yoona: il-la paç-çan min
beesha.

Mid-til de-di-lukh hai mal-choota oo khai-la
oo

Tush-bookh-ta l'alam al-mein. Aa-meen.

VERSION TWO

Our heavenly Father, hallowed is your name.
Your Kingdom is come.

Your will is done, As in heaven so also on
earth.

Give us the bread for our daily need. And
leave us serene,

Just as we also allowed others serenity. And
do not pass us through trial, except
separate us from the evil one.

For yours is the Kingdom, the Power and the
Glory To the End of Days, For all of the
universes. Amen!

VERSION THREE

Avinu sheba-shamayyim yitkadash shemaycha
Tavo malkutaycha yeasseh retzoncha k'mo
Ba-shamayyim kain ba-aretz et lechem

Hukaynu ten-lonu ha-yom u-slach lonu et
Hovotheynu ka-asher solachnu gam anachnu
L'ha-yavaynu vih-al tivi-aynu li-y'day nisa-
    yon
Kee im hal-tzaynu min harah

PRAYER TO ST. MICHAEL

The Prayer to St. Michael (the Archangel) is
originally part of a more elaborate exorcism rite
that was once performed at the end of each
Catholic Mass, after the induction of the
tradition by Pope Leo XIII. The full version can
be found in reprints of the Roman Roccolta
(1898), though use of it disappeared in the
1960's under the Second Vatican Council. There
is also a Chaplet of Devotion in Honor of St.
Michael and the Nine Choirs of Angels, also
known as the Angelic Chaplet.

The functional use of the chaplet was given to a
devout servant Antonia D'Astonac during a
personal apparition of St. Michael. In 1851,
Pope Pious IX granted significant indulgences
to all who use/pray the Chaplet ritual. During
the use of the Chaplet, the "Lord's Prayer" is
actually invoked before saluting each of the
Nine Choirs (angles) of Angel.

A left-hand version of this appears among Anton La-Vey's *Satanic Rituals*, called the Ceremony of Nine Angles and it is curiously listed in the "Metaphysics of Lovecraft" section of his book. Even those like LaVey have sought in bringing to light a practical side of what he hails as Lovecraft's Necronomicon and the Cthulhu-mythos. Curiously both the Simon *Necronomicon* and the LaVey works remain among the top selling occult materials of our time (and from the same publisher).

PRAYER TO ST. MICHAEL
– SHORT VERSION

> Saint Michael the Archangel, defend us
>   in battle, be our
> Protection against the wickedness and
>   snares of the devil.
> May God rebuke him we humbly pray;
>   and do thou,
> O Prince of the Heavenly Host, by the
>   Power of God,
> Cast into Hell, Satan and all the evil
>   spirits who prowl
> About the world seeking the ruin of
>   souls.
> Amen.

PRAYER TO ST. MICHAEL
– SHORT VER. (LATIN)

Sancte Michael Archangele, defende nos in
praelio.
Contra nequitiam et insidias diaboli esto
praesidium.
Imperet illi Deus, supplices deprecamur.
Turque princeps militiae caelestis, Satanam
aliosque spiritus malignos, qui ad
perditionem   animarum pervagantur in
mundo divina virtute
in infernum detrude.
Amen.

PRAYER TO ST. MICHAEL
– BANNED VERSION

O Glorious Prince of the heavenly host, St.
Michael the Archangel,
Defend us in the battle and in the terrible
warfare
That we are waging against the Principalities
and Powers,
Against the Rulers of this World of Darkness,
Against the evil spirits. Come to the aid of
man, whom Almighty God created
immortal,

Made in His own image and likeness,
And redeemed at a great price from the
        tyranny of Satan.

Fight this day the battle of the Lord, together
        with the holy Angels,
As already you have fought the leader of the
        proud Angels,
Lucifer, and his minions, who were powerless
        to resist Thee,
Nor was there place for them any longer in
        Heaven.
That cruel, ancient serpent, who is called the
        devil or Satan
Who seduces the whole world,
Was cast into the abyss with his Angels.

Behold, this primeval enemy and slayer of
        men has taken courage.
Transformed into an angel of light, he
        wanders about
With All the multitude of wicked spirits,
        invading the Earth
In order to blot out the name of God
And of His Christ, to seize upon,
Slay and cast into eternal perdition souls
        destined
For the crown of eternal glory.

This wicked dragon pours out, as a most
       impure flood,
The venom of his malice on men of depraved
       mind
And corrupt heart,
The spirit of lying, of impiety, of blasphemy,
And the pestilent breath of impurity, and of
       every vice
And iniquity. Arise then, O Invincible Prince,
Bring help against the attacks
Of the lost spirits to the people of God,
And give them the victory.

They venerate thee as their protector and
       patron;
You alone are our sole defense against the
       malicious power of Hell;
To thee has God entrusted the souls of men
To be established in heavenly beatitude.

Oh, pray to the God of Peace
That He may put Satan under our feet,
So far conquered that he may no longer be
       able to
Hold men in enslavement.
Offer our prayers in the sight of the Most
       High,
So that they may quickly find mercy in the
       sight of The Lord;

And vanquishing the dragon, the ancient
    serpent,
Who is the devil and Satan,
Do thou again make him captive in The abyss,
That he may no longer seduce the nations.
    Amen.

NECRONOMICAL SPELLCRAFT

Perhaps one of the most often exploited aspects of the Simon *Necronomicon* as a grimoire, is the *Book of Marduk*, which is to say the Babylonian Book of Fifty Names, adapted from the seventh (secret) tablet of the Babylonian Enuma Elis (called the "Magan Text" in the Simon *Necronomicon*). This was later revised by the editing team as the *Necronomicon Report* and then the *Necronomicon Spellbook*, which suggests using the ma-gick circle of operations and the Book of Fifty Names for spellcraft.

Sitting before the sigil/seal of the spirit/Gate, meditate and focus on the symbolism, focus on the goal of the working at hand and see it clearly in your mind (observ-ing the basic rules and techniques of low magickal ritual spell-craft). When working with spiritual entities and intelligences, the magician is instructed to focus on the current or vibration sought to make contact with. This includes not only the use of relevant symbols, but also "magick words" or "sacred names" which can be intoned repeatedly, including all "names of calling." Using the traditional formula found on arcane Chaldean, Akkadian and Babylonian tablets, the priest or magician would speak:

> *By the powers of Light & Darkness,*
> *By the powers of Heaven & Hell,*
> *ZI KIA KANPA. ZI DINGIR KIA KANPA.*
> * [Spirit of the Earth, remember (conjure it)!]*
> *ZI ANNA KANPA. ZI DINGIR ANNA KANPA.*
> * [Spirit of the Sky, remember (conjure it)!]*
> *Spirit N. come to me by the powers of the*
> *   word N.*
> *It is not I, but MARDUK, that summons thee*
> *   here.*

MESOPOTAMIAN LORE

The word ZONEI is related to the planets of fixed orbits. The mythic cycles were reduced to the seven-fold system because those were the planets still observable from Earth. While the lore of others still remained, it didn't make sense to calculate the effects of planetary bodies you weren't actually able to observe! ANUN-AKI is also spelled ANUNNAKI and is most often translated as "heaven meets earth" or "from heaven to earth," and typically becomes the "fallen angels" in contemporary lore.

Another permutation, ANU-NAGI denotes "star-dra-gon" (naga). Traditionally, AN denotes "star," "heaven" and "God" synonymously, which makes for difficult interpretations for the average cowan scholar. KI is equated with "Earth" or the physical world and thus, AN-KI combined is "heaven-earth" or "Universe." In Sumerian mythology, AN is objectified as ANU and KI becomes the consort of ANU, also known as ANTU.

The Control Center in Babylon was called E.TEMEN. AN.KI or "House of Foundation of Heaven & Earth" which is sometimes written E.TEMEN.ANA.KIA. A race of "Watchers" also appear in the tradition as the IGIGI, those who "observe & see," In Judeo-Christian lore it is Shamihaza who is leader of the two-thirds of the angels that fall from Heaven and concurrently in Mesopotamian lore, it is Shamgaz who brings 200 of the 300 IGIGI to Earth to take Daughters of Men as wives.

THE WATCHER-IGIGI CEREMONY

The Watcher or IGIGI ceremony is an archaic rite of apparently Mesopotamian origin that is suggested within the Simon *Necronomicon*. This ritual conjures a powerful guardian and protective entity that serves the will of the operator. Associated with the IGIGI-ANUN-NAKI and Nephilim-Elohim lore, the race of Watchers is apparently actually separate from that of men and Sky Gods [Elder Gods]. Initial contact is required to develop a relationship with the Watcher and monthly sacrifices must be made to retain this connection. It should be understood very clearly that blood offerings are never offered to the spirit. The sacrifice intended is agricultural as was originally done in the ancient shrines and temples of the ANUNN-AKI, including "new bread" (grain), resin from the pine tree (or true cedar) and nettle (called "olieribos").

The offering is burned in a cauldron called the *Aga Mass Ssaratu*, which is set between two concentric flour-marked circles, in the north-east. The operation is traditionally performed outdoors during the darkest hour of night (preferably during a new moon or eclipse). Some wizards begin such operations around midnight peak; others prefer the mystique of the 3:00 AM threshold. The operator should wear a black robe/cloak and Phrygian cap (conical hat) or hood. The wizard should also carry a sword bearing the Elder Sign on the hilt as well as the Copper shiv/dagger of Inanna. Some revivalists have opted to possess the "Jewels of the Gods" for ceremonial operations as well, particularly the essence of Lapis Lazuli.

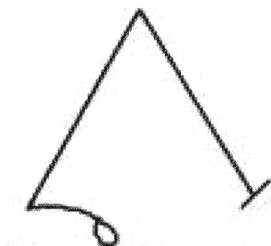

The first "Evocation of the Watcher" is used for the preliminary contact and first sacrifice. The Watcher may be consequently called each successive month (new moon?) with the second version, perhaps to coincide with the seeker's self-initiation upon the "Ladder of Lights" [Also called "Starwalking" or "Gatewalking" as each rung of the ladder (or Gate) corresponds with a "star").

The sword is thrust into the ground once the incantation is complete and should remain untouched until the operation is completed (which should then be removed with the following words: *"Barra Mass Ssaratu. Barra"*]. One version of the rite suggests the pointing of the blade or dagger of Inanna upwards during the incantation. Prior to conjuring the Watcher, the ritual fire should be conjured/consecrated to GIBIL, God of the fire and GIRRA, Spirit of the Fire with the words:

GIBIL Gashru Umuna Yanduru
Tushte Yesh Shir Illani U Ma Yalki!
Gishbar Ia Zi Ia. Ia Zi
Dingir GIRRA Kanpa!

PRELIMINARY EVOCATION
OF THE WATCHER

Iss Mass Ssarati Sha Mushi Lipshuru
Ruxisha Limnuti. Izizanimma Ilani
        Rabuti
Shima Ya Dababi. Dini Dina Alakti
        Limda.
Ku Nushi Ilani Mushiti.
Ia Mass Ssarati. Iss Mass Ssarati.
Ba Ids Mass Ssaratu.

EVOCATION OF THE WATCHER

Ia Mass Ssaratu.
I conjure thee by the Fire of GIRRA,
The veils of the sunken Varlooni,
And by the Lights of SAMAS.
I call there here before me, in visible
*   shadow,*
In beholdable form, to watch and protect
*   this*
Most sacred mandala, the Holy Gate of
*   N.*
He of the unspeakable name,
The unspeakable number, whom no man
*   has seen*
At any time, whom no geometer has
*   measured,*
Whom no wizard has ever called,
I call thee here now.
Rise up. By ANU, I summon thee.
Rise up. By ENLIL, I summon thee.
Rise up. By ENKI, I summon thee.
Cease to be the Sleeper of E.GURRA.
Cease to lie dreaming beneath the
*   Mountains of KUR.*
Rise up, from the dark pits of ancient
*   holocausts.*
Rise up, from the ancient abyss of NARR
*   MARRATU.*

Come by ANU. Come by ENLIL.
Come by ENKI.
In the name of the sacrificial covenant,
Come and rise up before me.
Ia Mass Ssaratu. Ia Mass Ssaratu.
Ia Mass Ssaratu.
Zi Kia Kanpa. Barragolomoloneth Kia.
Shtah.

THE LOST BOOKS

OF

MERLYN STONE

MARDUKITE
CHAMBERLAINS

EDITOR'S PREFACE

During the 1990's the public interest in 'magick' and the 'occult' doubled – if not tripled or even quadrupled, exponentially rising to new heights that few could have anticipated. The amount of "New Age" material being published *soared* – the companies and creators that produced them had the ability to, for the first time in contemporary history, develop significant and legitimate income based on the "New Age."

Now, someone reading this is going to quickly argue about all of the developments that they may have experienced in the 1960's, and further still, we have the blossoming of occult lodges that became publicly visible during the turn of the 20th century – factions such as the *Golden Dawn* and hermetic schools of *Theosophy* that are now over 100 years old in their founding. I am certainly not going to deny the existence of these things – but lets face it, the occult revival has only just recently passed its infancy, and that is why it has had so many growth spurts, though it still exists to simply test its own limits and get a feel for its skin... While this is all changing now, existing in an ever-shifting face of reality.

I appeared on the "New Age" scene, however much 'underground' in 1995 as "Merlyn Stone." As I have explained to others and in my recent autobiographical narrative, *Nabu Speaks!*, the name was chosen for personal reasons and not as a tribute to the female author (Merlin Stone) of whom I had not even heard of at that time.

The name "Merlyn" is not really a proper name, although it has been used to refer to particular figures (or *a* figure) in history, it is actually a title – a *Welsh title* – that can be best equated to what you might know as a *seer* or *prophet*. The contemporary reader may be more familiar with the Judeo-Christian religious context of the title, which in Hebrew is *nabih*, derived from the Babylonian name: *Nabu*.

I prefer the semantic of the *seer*, because to the modern mind, this idea of "prophet" is probably going to be lost on people – raising defenses unnecessarily and causing the *messages* to be lost. For that matter, I would prefer the concept of a *messenger* who is simply carrying a certain message as opposed to a *prophet* who is privy to unique and secret information that no one else is in possession of. While the later may be true to a certain extent, such might also apply to all people and times.

228

During only the three decades of my current existence in the physical realm I have watched as "crystal healers" went from working in basements in the 1980's to having fully leased and store-fronted offices. I have watched as the thousands who once only reserved themselves to secluded monthly meetings and the study of books in closets by candlelight now wear their full regalia in public places reserved for large festivals and parades.

Don't get me wrong – I understand that many of you have endured suffering still to this day for your inclinations toward a "mystical," "occult" or otherwise "pagan" *living philosophy*. There are still more who are unable to exist in this freedom I have just described, worried for the very real repercussions and animosity that can come from work or family – lives in this *system* can be lost or laid to ruin. Believe *me*, I fully *understand*. But... times are changing *still*.

The height of the 1970's and early 1980's really paved the way – cushioning the *societal* blow that comes with large 'paradigm-shifts'. Among these was, of course, the Simon *Necronomicon* that appeared in 1977, the same year as *Star Wars* and the birth of the *Shannara* epic by Terry Brooks.

Mainstream consciousness was being upgraded, and with it the *guise* was usually always something other than what it *appeared* to be. This is often the case in the 'material realm'. While there were the more obvious introductions of semantics born from *Dungeons and Dragons*, and related *fantasy* enthusiasm, the children of the 80's were also being prepped – their minds opened to new realms of possibility that were veiled in the paradigms of their parental generations. In the introduction to *Merlyn's Magick* (2005), I refer to the mystical and magical themes coming into focus with the cult interest in such aspects as *The Dark Crystal*, *Care Bears*, *Labyrinth* and the like. While an entire book could be (and probably has) been written on the contributions of the psychedelic new age 'hippie' towards this change in consciousness, it will suffice for our purposes of its mere mentioning here.

As far as I could observe, however, it was 1995 that provided the largest shift. I took a step back, observing the wide-angle, and I saw the prominence of the newly released motion picture *The Craft* coupled with *Sabrina the Teenage Witch* as the featured 'after-school-special' of the day. Clearly the coast was clear and it was time to come out – come *awake!*

While I was not alone in hearing this 'call', the work I had to do – the *program* I was here to follow – was not something readily understandable to the population – even a "New Age" one. The plans were laid before I ever showed up in this life, but patience was key as was watching for the signposts and keeping my head down. It was going to take everything to bring the work to the heights it can now be found in, but in the 1990's, the world was not ready for what I had to say concerning the origins of 'magick' and the "mardukite" legacy, so I had to start at the beginning – to build a basis – to work from the foundation rock or *stone*.

All of my original 'writings' related to the occult field were actually the subject of 'in-house' materials being prepared for working groups and research oriented studies that I was personally involved with – and often the 'founder' of. I began this work publicly in 1995 and it has now been over 15 years since – half of my current existence. It has taken many forms, though it was easiest for me to begin with that which would be most familiar to my target demographic: *esotericists, occult practitioners* and the up and coming *alien youth* that usually had inclinations toward the "New Age" naturally.

In 1995, the world was not ready for *Marduk-ites*. I worked within the paradigms that were much more accessible and did not require a lot of background – *ritual magick, spellcraft, high psychology* and even the *ceremonial* systems. The two methodologies I was most concerned with in connecting the later work I had hoped to accomplish (now known as the *Mardukites*) was the *Pheryllt Druid* material of Douglas Monroe and also "Simon's" *Necronomicon*.

This was about as close as I could come to 'mainstream', and even *these* facets of the "New Age" had been enshrouded in misguided controversy and restricted recommendations from the more publicly elite and visible organizations and group leaders. "Members" were explicitly told *not* to look into these materials, just as much as the current *Mardukite* work has seen its share of scrutiny and disapproval from the uninitiated. It came as no surprise then that the only work I had done during this period that survived in the mainstream was probably the most 'commercially' viable of the "Merlyn Stone" titles and that is the *Sorcerer's Handbook.*, now celebrating its 13th anniversary in circulation across *8 editions* not including the 2005 release of *Merlyn's Magick*, of which it was the basis.

INTRODUCTION

As I explained in the epilogue of the *Necronomicon of Merlyn Stone*, When I first started out, I assisted in the development of the *Druid Compleat* under the 'Sacred Grove Press', which was the in-house handbook for the *Draconis Celtic Lodge of Druids* (in Denver). I was 13 years old... I continued by literary career with the premiere release of the *Sorcerer's Handbook*, which was connected to a transition from *DCLOD* to the underground group that formed as a result of the publications (going the other direction) known as the *Order of the Crystal Dawn*, which led to the use of the name 'Crystal Dawn Press'.

In the midst of these efforts, running from 1995 through 1999, a separate group was founded to 'playtest' a teenage version of the *Sorcerer's Handbook*, called *Young Sorcerer*, and the work of this group expanded the need for further literary compilations connected to it, mainly *Crystalline Awakening* and the aforementioned *Necronomicon of Merlyn Stone*. My participation with this special group (the *Elven Fellowship Circle of Magick*) actually overlapped with the formation of the *Order of the Crystal Dawn*.

This is when things became challenging for me and I was forced to burrow into the underground from 2001 up until the founding of the *Mardukites* in the summer of 2008. While I was 'away', *Merlyn's Magick* appeared on the scene in 2005, written under my 'given' name, Joshua Free and alluding to a mysterious figure who had made an appearance then suddenly disappeared – *Merlyn Stone*.

The deeper the work reached – the closer it was getting to what I am now known for – the more difficult it was to reach people. The transition toward 'states of consciousness' and 'embracing euphoria' as described in *Crystalline Awakening* were actually wholly edited for commercialized acceptance and barely even reflected the tones I was stressing in the original draft (that was used by the *Elven Fellowship Circle of Magick* in 1999) titled *Crystalline Sphere*. What the work was attempting to illustrate has almost become hum-drum now over a decade later, but at the time my readership was not ready to hear it – at least not from me.

In 2009 a small print run was released exclusively to the "Mardukite Chamberlains" to companion to the re-release of the *Sorcerer's Handbook* at that time. The small anthology excerpted from several 'unpublished' (publicly) and underground creations designed (again) for in-house use originally. *The Pocket Book of Druidry* (1995) and *Upon Druid Hills at Midnight* (1996) were both prepared for the pre-*DCLOD* project I had going in Minneapolis called *Mystics of the Earth* along with the first edition of the *Draconomicon* (which is being revisited, revised and expanded upon for a future occult literary project by some interested *Mardukites*).

The "Archives" have just been moved three times in as many years and are actually being prepared to be moved again – in addition to being broken up and distributed among several underground figures. In doing so, we found a box that had been sealed for a decade, concealing the original 'galley proofs' for the works just listed along with the original *Crystalline Sphere* discourse, the *Necronomicon of Merlyn Stone* and a notebook labeled *Macht* (German for "power") that is dated 1998. Given the resurgence of interest toward the "pre-Mardukite" *Merlyn Stone* works I developed in my youth, I am pleased to prepare this "Lost Books" companion to the re-released *Sorcerer's Handbook!*

~ Nabu Joshua Free (*Merlyn Stone*)
Summer 2011

**MARDUKITE
CHAMBERLAINS**

MERLYN'S DRUIDRY

The *Druids* were historically a learned group of men and women made popular during the "ancient" *Celtic* times. They formed their own communities in *Keltia*, what we more commonly know as Ireland, Britain and Gaul (now France). Their counsel and wisdom was sought out by many different groups of people and societies, particularly when some mediation was required.

With much unhappiness I can easily say that the majority of the public texts involving the ancient *Druids* was documented or based on documents of the ancient *Romans*, who were notoriously the archenemy of the *Druids*. With this in mind, there is not much we can take for granted (or at the very least, unbiased) from these *Roman* accounts.

After all, if we were responsible for preserving the memory of our enemies, how might we go about coloring this with our attitudes?

It is well known that the *Druids* held the Oak Tree as sacred, as well as the herb referred to as "mistletoe." Both *herbs* make frequent appear-

237

ances in *Druidic* rituals. It has become fairly well propagated knowledge, as well, that human sacrifices played some prominent role in their tradition as well.

With the coming of Christianity, *Druidism* faced its final days with the 'fall of the elves' and the donation of the Roman Empire by Emperor Constantine to the establishment of the "Vatican" *Catholic Church*. The 'End of Days' for the *Druids* appeared to have come about in the sixth century, when it disappeared for a time...

...but here we are now in the 20th century, going into the 21st [We are, of course, now in the 21st century at the time of printing. -Ed.] *Druidism* and *neopaganism* has begun to once again play a significant role in modern culture.

It appears to have made a reappearance in the public's eye sometime in the 1400's and 1500's, when *Druidism* was being studied by medieval historians and the first 'books' were written on the topic (post-*Romana*) explaining what was found from these studies. Lost manuscripts were being discovered in obscure places and many ancient writings were being deciphered by 'antiquarians'.

In the 1600's and 1700's, colleges and universities in Europe were beginning to study this revived interest in the *Druids* more academically. *Lost books* containing ceremonies and rituals in varying European languages became the subject of interpretation among people from all walks of life.

By the late 1800's and beginning of the 1900's, the word was spreading quickly about the revivalist traditions and systems of *Druidry* – and looking back we can see the period where the majority of what we academically learned about the *Druids* became solidified in public consciousness was during this time. What had begun as the uncovering of a myth was developing into a historical natural living religion.

English, Welsh and Irish nationalist founded a new order of *Druids* for modern times, calling themselves the "Ancient Order of Druids." They set our to revive their own practical interpretation of the ancient *Druid* tradition – even reclaiming *Stonehenge* in the name of the *Druids* and observing public ceremonies there as often as possible.

Soon after, because of tourism, *Stonehenge* began to show increasing signs of damage and the landowners decided to begin charging an entrance fee in order to offset maintenance costs. When the AOD showed up and refuse to pay, they were arrested accordingly for misconduct.

In the 1930's the name of the revival changed to the "Ancient Order of Druid Hermeticists" – a membership that was composed of ex-AOD members by eighty percent. The AODH devised their own newsletter magazine titled *Pendragon*. By 1955 only one of the original five chapters of the AODH still existed – they even claimed to be the sole survivors practicing of the original Ancient Order of Druids (AOD).

A NEW DRUID ORDER

Surely, when someone hears the word "new," it probably means to them that it is 'not the original'or that the concept is 'wholly new'. The *neo-*movement found within this current age is not really new at all, but tends to work from the most favorable and widely used sources that within themselves will often make claims of *originality*.

I would estimate that the average "New Ager"

easily can accumulate a collection of books averaging between $50-500 within their first year of mild-to-average avid research and study. While they will most likely still lack the materials often necessary for serious advancement, the second year will often times be spent putting hundreds of dollars into buying and/or makign ritual tools and other 'mystical' bric-a-brac, often before the full understanding of what the item represents has been fully realized.

The *Druids* were magicians, though, but they were also poets and musicians, healers and shamans, statesmen and politicians. In the early days of the *Celts* and *Druids*, the sacred sites and 'stone circles' were sought for their ability to assist in the reverence of Nature and the "Source of All" and the same was not destroyed for the purpose of building artificial churches, a celebration of the means of men more than a God.

Even though *Druidism* appeared to 'die' with the coming of Christianity, the practices continued to covertly survive embedded in the works of *Bardic Schools*, which were able to make contributions with remnants still found today in British, Welsh and Irish traditions.

241

Unlike ever before in the current age, there is actually a dire need for the *Druids* to make a return in our civilization today – regardless if they are in one-to-one reflection with the 'classical' image of *Druidry*. But, nonetheless, the fate of the planet seemingly depends on this very presence, under whatever semantics is being observed to represent the *Guardians of the Old Ways* – true stewards of the very face of the earth itself.

Clearly, if this way of thinking is not for you, then it should never be forced. It is a living tradition that comes from the *stars* – and the blood of those who are called and chosen to bare the title also come from the *stars*.

What is being described here are the same mysteries that have been explored from the beginning of modern civilization, the inception of the *Dragon Kings* of *Mesopotamia* and their spread across *Eurasia*, through the 'Holy Lands' and Magan desert, Egyptian Nile, Asia and India, the Siberian mountains, the European mainlands, the aboriginal traditions of southern, central and northern America.... all of this can be traced and linked back to the Source.

Those who are coming forth, awakening in this

modern world, are feeling the call towards the 'something' that has brought us here in this time and place to serve a function that exists outside of time and space...

...we have not long to wait for the realization of our purpose: the uncovering and resurrection of the true source tradition from which we first emerged on this planet, which has been hidden from human sight and left to the politics of self-serving covert organizations to control.

...that time has ended.

…and a new era is in our midst.

THE DRUIDESS

There are several related texts that speak of *dryades*, *dryads* and *druidesses* – each of these seemingly denoting a *female druid*, or *daughter of the forest*.

Although it follows a completely different para-digm on the duality of opposites, *wicca* appears to be relatively similar to the 'natural' path of *Druidry* – it appears to be more commonly sought by New Age *females*. It is not uncommon to find *Druids* and *wiccans* getting together for mutual practices and gatherings.

Contrary to the view held by the *Celts* themselves, the Romans looked upon women simply as second-class citizens that could have children and be objects of pleasure. The *Druids* actually included women in their political and religious lifestyles as equals.

The idea of female magicians is usually supported by the conceptualization of a *witch* – and as a matter of speaking, a female *druidess* could indeed be thought of as a *witch*. But, here's the kicker – in modern nomenclature, the male *druid* is also able to be considered a *witch* – mainly because the semantics of *warlock* seem to have too negative of overtones to be functional in a 'PC' world. The title of *green witch* or *earth witch* can also be found.

There is popular *Celtic* lore describing the *Druidess* and their abilities to raise storms, cause diseases and kill enemies with supernatural curses, as alluded to in *Celtic* mythology and *Bardic* histories.

THE DRUID "RELIGION"

There are over three-hundred names of earth deities and sky gods given in the literature of the *Celts* and *Druids* – though it has been unfortunately been misinterpreted as polytheism in the sense of "worship" (by current historians and naïve mythologists).

Druids were thought of as an ambassador or intermediary between the population of humans and the 'sky gods', or else the bridge between the mortal and immortal realms – that which is seen versus that which is unseen – and yet they, themselves, understood the great mysteries that all-is-one and there is only one reality, central, united and equal to the entire material world (described in their *cabala*) experienced from *self*.

The idea that *druids* literally "worship" Nature is ridiculous, as should be clear by any modern practitioner or revivalist. *Druids* viewed Nature as the untouched representation of the Creator or "creative force" of the Universe, that which was essentially the united Source of All Being and Creation. The source can be found within and as the natural creation of the source and not the creations of man, who misinterprets his own creative natures.

Classical *druidry* alludes to mystical abilities, such as calling (summoning) and commanding the *shades* (or 'soul imprint') of discarnate (ascended) *Druids* (of one's ancestors). These rites of the dead have caused many 'darker' overtones.

Druids, as 'shamans', made frequent 'astral journeys' to the Otherworld – using this means to encounter and work with the natural energies that exist beneath the perceptions in the more solid physical realm. This is not altogether different than what is described in the practices of indigenous shamans in other cultures.

The ability to communicate with trees and nature spirits played a large part not only in the naturalistic lifestyle of the *druid* but also the oracular magick performed as what is now called 'divination'. One method of such is by use of the "Ogham" system which is said to have been given to the *Druids* by the *Elven-Faerie*.

A link to the natural world was also maintained through regular work with both physical and spiritual forms of sacred (power) animals – and this communicative link with the nautral world also allowed energetic resonances to be radiated and felt (as part of nature) even at great distances.

DRUIDIC DIVINATION METHODS

Divination by use of the three dark stones...

...according to lore, a bucket of coal was sent to the priests when they were unsure of a man's truth. In this bucked of coal was placed a black stone, a white stone and a speckled stone. Then, one in question would put his hand into the bucket and if the truth was with him he would pull from it the white stone. If he was false, he would pull the black stone and if he was partially guilty he would pull the speckled stone.

Divination by use of the earth runes...

...was used quite often in the Celto-Norse region, just as scarabs and other cuneiform oracles were used in the Mesopotamian region. The Viking Runes are the Celtic Ogham have come to be used by New Age practitioners in the same manner.

Divination by use of the Triscale Stones...

...requires three stones: a hematite for the silver stone, an obsidian for the black stone (or coal can be used) and pyrite (or tiger's eye) for the gold stone. You can also search for natural stones that are of a similar color, for example: yellow for gold and blue for silver.

When you ask your question, often before a sacred "Oracle Tree," throw the stones in front of you on a flat surface. The black stone is the indicator and the one closest to it "indicates" the answer – the gold stone for "yes" and the silver for "no."

FOUNDATIONS OF THOUGHT

We've all heard of the *Druids*. How much do you *really* know about them, though? The classic image of a circle of white-robed wizards who gather at *Stonehenge* is immediately conjured to mind. Beyond that, there is the image crafted at Hollywood...

...two teenage *Druids* must prevent the son of Satan from using runestones to bring about the end of the world (*Warlock 2: The Armageddon*).

...a *Druid* nanny must sacrifice newborn babies

to her sacred tree, which has the powers to protect and heal her (*The Guardian*).

...a tribe of *Druid* shamans, who drink orange soda, dominate a tropical island possessing an active volcano that requires an occasional sacrifice (*Joe vs. Volcano*).

Unfortunately there has been a lack of decent materials for the aspiring modern *Druids*. Most of the books available are rehashes of their questionable history. Fewer resources will relate to the reader something pragmatic and practical for our times – again, unfortunate.

If you are somewhat experienced or previously schooled in things *druidic*, it is possible that my forthcoming message may surprise you – in regards to three important aspects.

1. There were *no* human sacrifices related to *Druidry* in Britain or Ireland. There is some evidence for this on mainland Europe, for example Gaul (now France). The Romans, whose tales are used by historians as a bible for learning of the *Druids*, had encountered and wrote of the *Druids* of Gaul before they invaded Britain. The accounts are extraordinarily biased and xenophobic in their interpretation.

2. The *Druidic* histories and lessons *were* written down. This was one of the many purposes of the *Ogham* script – in addition to using the 'tree alphabet' to arrange 'forest libraries' consisting of dried leaves. The *Druids* also knew how to apply the *Ogham* to hand signals and gestures giving them a silent 'sign-language'. Romans sought to destroy all the evidence that the *Druids* existed and their legions of soldiers were fed with a new-found 'fire' when invading the *Celts*. Julius Caesar once even recounted that the *Druids* had put up the most resistance to an invasion than any other culture encountered by the Roman Empire.

3. *Druidism never* was, nor should it be, considered a "religion" in the context that the word is used in contemporary society. It can be better examined as a "fraternity," "brotherhood," or "secret society," with an equally significant *Celtic*-based "sorority" known as the Motherhood of Avalon. Such organizations *still* exist and they share a long lineage of participation with various 'secret orders'.

Druids are an interesting archetype. For all of recorded time, there has always been someone or some group claiming to be *druidic*. In spite of this, or maybe because of it, the hardcore lineage and true sources of practical modern *Druidry* are difficult to ascertain. In many ways, *Druidry* can be best described as a *niche* – it seems to come naturally, and people are naturally inclined or drawn toward it or not.

THREE CHIEF DOCTRINES

Although many will often depict the *Druid* materials as 'religious dogma', the doctrines and core fundamentals of *druidry* do not appear to be such. In uncovering the *doctrines* there are few resources that provide clarity, one of them being Douglas Monroe's debut book *The 21 Lessons of Merlyn* – and while some of the larger public possessions have been to *not* read this work, that is not the attitude of the current editor.

Doctrine of Critical Periods: Children possess a unique learning capability which disappears in adulthood.

It is now known that the *Druids* were the educators of all the children in *Keltia*. Children who showed the most promise or who were from the appropriate 'bloodlines' were sent to a separate place of *druidic* schooling. Traditionally, at one point in history, the females were sent to *Avalon* and the males to the *Isle of Iona*, of the coast of Britain. There is also evidence of elite *Druid* activity on the small island directly below Britain, named the *Isle of Wight* or *ynys wyth* – the *Druids* knew as "Dragon Island."

W. Winwood Reade, in his history of the *Druids*, explains that *Celtic* parents often did not receive their children until they were fourteen years old – after they had first been reared by the learned *Druids*.

<u>Doctrine of Authority</u>: The quest is of authority of the Self, and through the Self, the authority of the world around us.

The *Druid* philosophy holds that what some would call 'magickal power' is really an authority or discipline executed from *Self*. Surely, they believed in *mind-over-matter* and were aware of 'psychosomatic' ills. They knew the physics of 'conservation' in that all life and energy possessed the ability to transcend all life as spirit – and this was extended to more than just *human* life.

Authority, like wisdom, is gained over time self-honestly, developed strong in the individ-

252

ual. In the ancient tradition, glass or stone beads were even awarded to an apprentice to show the completion of certain lessons. These were hung on a cord and carried (or worn) as symbols of universal authority. The nature of the *Druid's* "power" suddenly become more clear.

Doctrine of Separations: A destructive inter-ference can occur in the development of mixed genders. In accordance with attraction, the ener-getic circuit can be disrupted.

Perhaps the most controversial of the doctrines for modern interpretation, this facet of *Pheryllt* materials has actually caused discordance of mixed-gender magick when related to Douglas Monroe's writings. However, the esoteric trad-itions required male and females to be schooled and housed separately.

Certainly there are times when mixed-gender energetic work was appropriate – and as such, the *Bardic College* and *Avalon* worked quite closely at the apex of the *Druid's* reign in *Keltia*. High ranking *Druid's* did become liken-ed to priests in their requirement of *spiritual continence* and *sexual abstinence*, though this was not required of all classes. The *Avalonians* dedicated their bodies as embodiments of the *goddess*, and as such generally reserved sexual practices for 'magickal' purposes.

CRYSTALLINE AWAKENING

Since the dawn of time, the Earth has been graced with our presence, the true *Guardians of the Earth* and stewards of the *Secrets of the Universe*. Sorcerers. Wizards. Mystics. Now is the time for us to emerge and awaken from our hiding places and greet the times, being what they are.

The *Sacred Order of the Crystal Dawn*, or rather what it represents, has been dormant for centuries, awaiting a time when the "wizard" might resume a rightful role in society – and it is a time of awakening where many will be bonding together (and coming apart) to once again partake in the *secret ceremonies*.

In accordance with the *Great Plan* of the *Illuminati*, I hereby open the book of the mysteries to the initiate.

CHAPTER DEFINITIONS

The Chapter: Hereby defined as a "fellowship" of members. The individual "chapters" must notify their "Grant Chapter" of their region concerning their existence. Only one "Grand Chapter" can operate in a particular state or region as defined by the "Home Office."

CHAPTER HEIRARCHY

NEOPHYTE – The *first degree* of the Crystal Dawn, represented by the small green (new growth) diamond as found in alchemical texts to represent the novice "puffer" on a red trian-gle (of the flaming spirit).

ENTERED APPRENTICE – A *second degree* initiate who has been allowed to partake in the "Awakening" ceremony after proper study and preparations. The grade is represented by the sign use by alchemists to represent salt (in blue) which looks like a scarab – representing the union and absolution of opposition, within an orange triangle.

ADEPT – A *third degree* initiate who has proven prowess in the magickal arts including the high ceremonial arts. The grade is represented by the black and white eclipse sign on a checkered triangle.

AWAKENED APPRENTICE – The *fourth deg-*

ree of the Crystal Dawn, also a *second degree "sorcerer's apprentice"* is reserved for an initiate in the mystical arts that extend outside the contemporary defined boundaries of "magick" and "wizardry," possibly including, but not limited to the practical uses of intuition and psionic abilities. The grade is represented by a red androgyne sign (of fusion) on a green triangle ("coming forth").

MASTER – A *fifth degree* initiate who has completed the introductory or 'educational' degrees preset by the Crystal Dawn, often taking as much as three years of work and study. The sign used to represent the grade is a purple all-seeing eye within a 'squared' blue circle (all of which is in a triangle). This is the sign of the *philosopher's stone*.

INITIATION

Entrance (admittance) to each degree is also supplemented by an initiation ceremony that is open to members in good standing who are of an equal degree or above (to that which the initiate is being installed to at that time).

DEGREE INSIGNIA USAGE

Each degree has a corresponding insignia as described with the listing of the grades. They can be constructed from cut-to-fit pieces colored fabric and attached to a sturdy black square (of any material) that is able to be worn or pinned. In formal ceremonies of the *Order of the Crystal Dawn*, members wore these on the left arm below the shoulder. In private practice, many wore them around their neck as a talisman of authority.

[These insignias no longer appear to be in use by the existing faction of *CD*, the *Mardukite Chamberlains*. -Ed.]

GENDER

The *Order of the Crystal Dawn* is open to initiates of both genders. While certain services or practices, areas of dressing, etc. may be restricted to certain genders at a given time. There is no bias made concerning gender abilities in the *Order*.

[This appears to have been upheld by the *Mardukite Chamberlains*. -Ed.]

SPONSORSHIP

To be granted membership (initiation) into a chapter, the candidate must be 'sponsored' with a 'referral' by an existing member in good standing with the *Order*. The sponsor must be present at the time of the initial installation (initiation) of the *Neophyte*.

[This fundamental has been upheld by the *Mardukite Chamberlains*. -Ed.]

INITIATION #1

This version is adapted from the *Elven Fellowship Circle of Magick* (EFCOM) *Book of Shadows* (BOS). Performance of the rite is prescribed to an outdoor nemeton (grove).

The initiate stands twenty-one steps from the eastern "ward" of the circle. They are blindfolded and their hands are tied behind their back (representing the bondage of the material world.)

The *sponsor* approaches the circle form the east and knocks three times (or rings a bell three times – the method varies).

LEADER: Who is it that knocks?

SPONSOR: I come with news of one who seeks to share in what we know and enjoy.

LEADER: Who vouches for this person?

SPONSOR: I do. S/he stands outside of our Circle, seeking entrance and installation.

LEADER: Bring him/her to me.

The *sponsor* leaves to retrieve the *initiate*, then returns and knocks again (etc.).

LEADER: Who is it that knocks?

SPONSOR: It is I *n.*, returning with the one who seeks to join us.

LEADER: What is his/her name?

The *sponsor* speaks the given 'birth name' to the leader.

LEADER: I address the *initiate* – Why is it that you would join us?

The *initiate* responds.

LEADER: I address the *sponsor* – Is the initiate properly prepared?

If the *sponsor* gives up an affirmative answer than the initiation ceremony continues. Otherwise it is ended and the *sponsor* is instructed to return with the *initiate* when they are properly prepared to accept *installation*.

LEADER: Therefore, I admit them to stand at our circle's center.

The *sponsor* leads the *initiate* to the center of the nemeton workspace.

LEADER: I address the *initiate* – Do you come here of your own 'free will', free from the bias or coercion of others?

INITIATE: I do.

LEADER: Therefore, we join hands around you that you will know the energies of our circle.

All *members* join hands in a circle around the *initiate*. The *leader* remains inside this 'band' with the *initiate*, walking around them clockwise while they continue the ceremony. The outer band moves counter-clockwise while producing a *humming/buzzing* sound.

LEADER: Know that this is our Sacred Circle of Fellowship and this Circle cannot be broken. You must *never* break our Circle of Fellowship. Do you swear?

INITIATE: I do.

The *Secret Rite of the Blade* is performed and then the initiation ceremony commences.

LEADER: Source of All-Being and Creation, Source of all Wisdom and Truth, Source of Love and Light, Source of Darkness and Depths of Existence, Great Powers of Menw and Awen, we beseech thee to be here now, witness and promote that in receiving this person into our circle, we may add strength to our Fellowship. May s/he help to lengthen our Golden Chain, that our powers may be enlarged to benefit all humanity, all life on earth and our honor to thee. Blessed be.

ALL: Blessed be.

LEADER: So mote it be. Shem-ham-phor-ash.

ALL: So mote it be. Shem-ham-phor-ash.

LEADER: So mote it be. IAO-AWEN.

ALL: So mote it be. IAO-AWEN.

The *sponsor* breaks circle and approaches the *initiate*.

LEADER: In removing the blindfold, know that you are entering the Light of Rebirth into our circle from a preexisting darkness of ignorance.

The *sponsor* removes the blindfold from the *initiate*.

LEADER: In removing the bindings, know that we release you from your captivity to an inherently evil worldly system of humanity.

The *sponsor* removes the bindings from the *initiate*.

LEADER: You are now a 'free person' and we greet you into our circle as such.

SPONSOR: (to the initiate with the *neophyte grip*, handshake) I Greet you as a free person.

All *members* present follow the *sponsor* in doing the same gesture. The *leader* is the last do do this.

INITIATION #2

The lodge of the chapter is prepared with the members standing in a circle nine feet in diameter around the leading *Master of the Craft*. The *sponsor* begins as one among them and the *initiate* is standing outside the door.

GUARD: Master of the Craft, there is an initiate awaiting entrance into the *n* degree of our *Order*.

MASTER: Who accounts for this candidate?

SPONSOR: I do. S/he stands outside the lodge seeking entrance to the *n* degree.

MASTER: Has the candidate been properly prepared for this degree?

SPONSOR: They have.

MASTER: Has the candidate been properly prepared for the initiation ceremony?

The *guard* leaves to be sure that the hands of the initiate are bound behind their back and that they are blindfolded.

The *sponsor* goes to the center of the circle to wait beside the *Master of the Craft*.

The *guard* knocks three times (or the number of times indicative to that degree in the appropriate pattern).

The *sponsor* goes and takes the *initiate* from the *guard* and leads them to stand at the center of the circle, in front of the *Master of the Craft*.

The *guard* remains by the door to the lodge.

MASTER: Is the initiate properly prepared?

SPONSOR: S/he is.

MASTER: Then the initiation shall commence. Guard, seal the door. Let no one interfere with these operations.

The *guard* locks the door to the lodge and then resumes their post near it.

MASTER: We may proceed.

SPONSOR: Master of the Craft, it is my honor to present this candidate for installation to the *n* degree of our Order. I present a petition that this candidate be allowed initiation to the *n* degree of this lodge, observed by the majority of the members here present.

MASTER: I address the *initiate* – What is it that you seek here from us this da.y (night)?

The *initiate* answers accordingly.

MASTER: Therefore, it is with great pleasure then, that we welcome you to the *n* degree of the *Order of the Crystal Dawn*. By the reputation of your sponsor and the recommendations made on your behalf from your brethren in the lodge, we are assured that you are befitting of the *n* degree of this lodge and that you will understand this sacred trust being bestowed upon you by this fellowship. Is there any reason why you would be unable to submit yourself to the confidence and commitment of this Order at this time?

The *initiate* answers accordingly.

MASTER: Those who come to this fellowship in self-honesty seek to be Self-Masters, assisting themselves and others to assist themselves in this quest. Do you understand what I have just said?

The *initiate* answers accordingly.

MASTER: To be an integral part of the Order is to accept the truth and power laden in the Self. You will seek to understand the true natures of the potential waiting to be unlocked within you. Today, you will (re)confirm the path of this potential by affirming that the existence and power of God is within and as you. Are you able to do so, here among and with your brethren?

The *initiate* answers accordingly.

MASTER: All present may repeat – Man is God.

ALL: Man is God.

MASTER: We are human.

ALL: We are human.

MASTER: We are gods.

ALL: We are gods.

MASTER: God is man.

ALL: God is man.

MASTER: I address the *initiate* – do you hereby pledge yourself to the *n* degree of the Order?

The *initiate* answers accordingly.

MASTER: Do you swear allegiance to the secrecy of the *n* degree of the Order?

The *initiate* answers accordingly.

MASTER: The *sponsor* may remove the bindings – in doing so know that you are being unbound to the potential of the *n* degree, free to pursue this potential.

The *sponsor* removes the bindings.

MASTER: The *sponsor* may remove the blindfold – in doing so know that you are seeing the *n* degree of our Order for the first time. With new eyes you will be free to see yourself and the potential therein. One cannot seek what they cannot see. So look ever closely and observe in self-honesty.

The *sponsor* removes the blindfold and then hands the degree insignia patch to the *Master of the Craft*.

MASTER: This is the insignia of the *n* degree that is being bestowed upon you now. By this degree shall we know you by.

The *sponsor* approaches the *initiate* to shake their right hand in the grip of the degree while placing their left hand on the initiate's right shoulder.

SPONSOR: I greet you as a free person of the *n* degree.

All *members* present follow in performing the same gesture, ending with the *Master of the Craft*.

MASTER: I now declare the installation of this candidate to the *n* degree as completed. *Guard* – release the locks on the door. It is finished.

ALL: So mote it be.

RITE OF THE LAW – MODERN VERSION

This ritual, in some versions, is called the Tier-drama, after the German word for "beast" or "wild animal." IT was allegedly invoked in 1776 for the founding of the Bavarian Illuminati. Rumor has it that it has a history in American Freemasonry. It is certainly a Masonic-like Gnostic ceremony used to awaken or embrace the polar shadow-self of humans, the chaotic side that is called the *blood of Kingu* in Mesopotamian lore concerning the genetic origins of modern humans.

In the original version used by the *Elven Fellowship Circle of Magick*, a precursor to the now existent *Order of the Crystal Dawn*, the members stand in a half circle around the depiction of the "Baphomet" – an insignia representative of *Enki*, made famous by medieval factions of the *Knights Templar*, etc. This is traditionally placed on the banner of the western wall, or east if more appropriate to the lodge arrangement.

The *guard* is posted at the door to the lodge and instructed to secure it. The door is locked and a bell is rung signaling that the lodge has been properly secured.

MASTER: I am the sayer of the law. Here comes those who are new to hear the law. I stand alone and illuminated to speak the law. Cruel are the punishments to those who break the law, those who seek to exist against the natural flow of the Universe. Nothing escapes the law.

The Tierdrama – Rex Talionis

MASTER: Some want to watch the things that move. Some want to tear with their teeth and claws. Some go out fighting. Some go out biting. Punishment is sharp and sure for those who act against the law. Say the words. Learn the law. Not to go on all fours. This is the law.

ALL: Not to go on all fours. That is the law.

MASTER: Not to tear at plants and trees. This is the law.

ALL: Not to tear at plants and trees. That is the law.

MASTER: Not to snarl or roar. This is the law.

ALL: Not to snarl or roar. That is the law.

271

MASTER: Not to show teeth or fangs. This is the law.

ALL: Not to show teeth or fangs. That is the law.

MASTER: Not to destroy our possessions and habitat. This is the law.

ALL: Not to destroy our possessions and habitat. That is the law.

MASTER: Not to kill without thought. This is the law.

ALL: Not to kill without thought. That is the law.

MASTER: Man is God.

ALL: Man is God.

MASTER: We are men.

ALL: We are men.

MASTER: We are gods.

ALL: We are gods.

MASTER: God is within and as Man.

ALL: God is within and as Man.

MASTER: Ours is the hand that creates. This is the law.

ALL: Ours is the hand that creates. That is the law.

MASTER: Ours is the hand that wounds. This is the law.

ALL: Ours is the hand that wounds. That is the law.

MASTER: Ours is the hand that heals. This is the law.

ALL: Ours is the hand that heals. That is the law.

MASTER: Ours is the serpent lightning flash. This is the law.

ALL: Ours is the serpent lightning flash. That is the law.

MASTER: Ours is the deep salty sea. This is the law.

273

ALL: Ours is the deep salty sea. That is the law.

MASTER: Ours is the stars in the sky. This is the law.

ALL: Ours is the stars in the sky. That is the law.

MASTER: Ours is the rulers of the land. This is the law.

ALL: Ours is the rulers of the land. That is the law.

MASTER: This is what is ours to have. This is what we are.

ALL: This is what is ours to have. This is what we are.

MASTER: The rite is ended but we remember.

ALL: We remember.

MASTER: It is finished.

ALL: So mote it be.

THE AWAKENING – MODERNIZED

The initiate is placed in a single room that has been cleared of all else but a single candle that they find already lit on their arrival. They are left to themselves – sealed in the room – for a predetermined period of time. No electrical devices or other sources of light are left within the room. The *initiate* is then left only to themselves to analyze, think, contemplate and with enough time alone, will eventually overcome the diverse programmed personalities and hopefully lose the same. This period might first be only for a few hours or so, but may eventually be extended to include several days or even a week.

The greatest power is that which is gained in the silence and the speech of wisdom is what is found in the silence – the vision and the voice and eventually the abyss.

When the leading *master* opens the door to complete the time period, the *initiate* is warmly welcomed and embraced.

Ancient versions of this rite have included the use of caves, labyrinth mazes and other forms of ritualistic extremes that will not be analyzed here.

The *Crystalline Awakening* is necessary for the initiate to enter the 'inner circle' of the *Order of the Crystal Dawn*. The *Awakening* performed for the Entered Apprentice, focused on the confrontation of the *Ego* program requires a shorter period of time than the same working used by an Awakened Apprentice, who is focused on the dissolution of the *Ego* program – or what is sometimes described as *Ego-loss* as a whole, but at they very least the clear programming of the identity.

LAW OF THE MIND

Shakespeare once wrote that "nothing is good or bad except that thinking makes it so." The law of the mind is none other than that: We are as we think we are.

Buddha said that "all that we are is the result of what we have thought." A later philosopher, Marcus Aurelius wrote "our life is as our thoughts have made it."

Continuing with the words of other great minds, Mohammed said that "whatever mishaps befall you in this life are the result of your thoughts and actions."

...and from the Judeo-Christian Bible we read that the "reality of heaven and hell come from a man's own heart."

Humans essentially have the ability to "create" in that they can make visible what is already there (in the all equals one) for times and places relative to experience.

One is affecting changes and influencing energetic movement, not actually 'creating something from nothing' as it were. Our thoughts and actions can easily be seen as having the ability to heal, help, harm or destroy. And everything we do manifest outwardly is a reflection of what is held within – since the two are one and the same.

A fairly common method of employing the "Law of the Mind" is the use of affirmations and mantras. This is not the same as simply "positive thinking" or "wishful thinking" - this is about moving energy in the direction you want it to go rather than just wishing it was.

To understand the difference, consider the following examples that compare 'thinking' versus 'willing' by way of affirmation.

(thinking) I want to be a better person.
(willing) I am a success in what I think and do.

(thinking) I wish I were feeling better.
(willing) I am vibrant with good health.

Your mind is programmed to display what it 'knows' or has been 'taught', but it is also under the control of your 'will' (whether or not you can actual maintain this control has to do with other programming).

Reality becomes what it is because your mind agrees with predilections of said reality. The truth is, you don't actually have to agree with what you are programmed to see. You can change it.

In most cases, these changes are changes in 'roles' on a physical level and are really superficial, only lending to the furthering of various personalities already programmed on the psyche. What is essentially happening in most "New Age" or otherwise "active psychological" methods is a 'consciousness upgrade', which may be applicable to the world at large but still may or may not be true in self-honesty.

A leading interpreter of *creative psychology*

named Walter Silverton once wrote that "our life is just like a mirror." We observe situations and conditions taking form exactly according to the thoughts we are constantly projecting into the 'creative mind'.

CEREMONY OF THE EQUINOX
(CRYSTAL DAWN VERSION)

In astronomical observations of ceremonial magick, the 'crystalline' balance of the earth planet in conjunction with the the solar force of this existence, is found in the spring and autumn equinox observed annually.

The 'crystalline' balance or harmonic vibration is indicative of a union or 'balance' of extreme forces that were brought into being when the universe was manifested as a world of duality – form and thought, removed from its oneness.on Light and dark. Sun and moon. The equionx is the union, balance and absence of extremity.

For the *CD* performance of the *Equinox Rite*, the *master* stands in the east and represents the 'middle pillar' (see the *Golden Dawn* rite of the same name in the *Sorcerer's Handbook of Merlyn Stone*).

The Adept stands in the north near the black pillar and the acting Deacon stands in the south by the white pillar. The acting Priest stands in the west leading the responses of the other chapter members gathered in attendance.

MASTER: Brothers and sisters of the *Order of the Crystal Dawn*, assist me now in the opening of the chapter for the Ceremony of the Equinox.

The *priest* knocks three times.

MASTER: Guard, seal the door to this lodge. Allow no one to interfere with this assembly.

The *guard* locks the door and remains nearby.

MASTER: State your positions.

ADEPT: Here I stand at the black pillar.

DEACON: Here I stand at the white pillar.

MASTER: I am the reconcile between them.

DEACON: I am the Fire – Chokmah – Yod.

PRIEST: I am the Water – Binah – Heh.

MASTER: I am the Air – Tiphareth – Vahv.

ADEPT: I am the Earth – Malkuth – Heh.

MASTER: Here we stand – here on this obser-
vance of the Equinox, witness to the sealing of
the Great Forces of Nature. Here we stand. Here
at the threshold of balance. *Beltiste. Soi ten
cardian. Didomi cathemerios. Phylaxomenen.*

ALL: Ee Oh Ee-voh-heh. Ah Oh Ee-voh-heh.
Ee Oh Ee-voh-heh.

ADEPT: *Alphito-Baitule Lusia Nonacris. Anna
Fearina Salmoana.*

ALL: Ee Oh Ee-voh-heh. Ah Oh Ee-voh-heh.
Ee Oh Ee-voh-heh.

DEACON: *Strabloe Athaneatidas ura druei.
Tanaous kolabreusomera.*

ALL: Ee Oh Ee-voh-heh. Ah Oh Ee-voh-heh.
Ee Oh Ee-voh-heh.

PRIEST: *Kirkotokous athroize te Mani. Grog-
opa gnathoi ruseis iota.*

ALL: Ee Oh Ee-voh-heh. Ah Oh Ee-voh-heh.

281

Ee Oh Ee-voh-heh.

MASTER: Soul of the Golden Sun, grant us strength, passion, joy and love. Soul of the Dark Moon, grant us inspiration, intuition, enchantment and knowledge.

ADEPT: Let the Crystalline Pillar shine bright in our hearts to balance our own powers and bestow wisdom.

DEACON: As we emerge into the world of form, let the radiance of the Crystal Dawn bring us all to a renewed Awakening.

The *priest* approaches the *master* and then proceeds to walk clockwise around the circle.

The *deacon* approaches the *master* and then proceeds to walk clockwise around the circle.

The *adept* approaches the *master* and then proceeds to walk clockwise around the circle.

The *master* follows the procession, closely behind the *adept*.

The remaining members of the *congregation* follow behind the *master* until until they have reached the boundaries of the lodge.

MASTER: Halt!

The procession stops.

MASTER: As we have come together in form-alities so too must we depart. May the *priest* aid me in closing the lodge chapter.

PRIEST: Guard, release the door. The chapter has been closed.

The *guard* unlocks the door.

PRIEST: It is finished.

ALL: So mote it be.

THE CODEX UNICORNIS

From the depths of the desert fathers came the Collegium Gnosticum, a secret brotherhood of hermetic mystics. Within the core of their teach-ings is a small piece known only as "Last Days" describing the prophecies of a 'paradigm-shift', which are also found in the Notebooks of Mag-nalucius. It states:

The Unicornis Prophecies

Behold, a day shall come when science will darken everywhere the hopes of men. Chariots of iron shall roll the land which has become barren and hard to bare their weight.

The air will be filled with with the clamor of many voices at once and unknown plagues and sickness will arise among the people. The sphere of the moon will bare the booted heels of the Race of Men.

Mighty kingdoms will compete for world control and they turn against the spirits of the soil, and the land and sea are sickened – the air carries poisonous vapors. All men will be tried and faced with their choice between the seen and the unseen.

Only then will come a Great Purification. The Unicorn returns, lingering at the margins of our realm, seeding the minds of the dedicated with the dreams and visions of a 'brighter' age to come – and there will be many who hunger to see the vision in those times. The image of the Unicorn, being spiritual, will only reside in the hearts of those who know it.

FORMULAE UNICORNIS

The ongoing fight between perceptible forces exists only in the physical world, for in the realm of the highest reality, all is oneness, and so we are plagued here in the physical to endure the dualistic forms that seek to achieve balance in this form – a balance that will never be gained in the physical world – and so they remain in systems of chaos formed into patterns.

The Notebooks of Magnalucius allude to *De Libro Nemeseos* – the "Book of Nemesis" (of which an ancient version, known as the *Enuma Elis* can now be found within the *Mardukite* core). One can see the later Gnostic and mystical attributes reflected in the Michael Green interpretation:

In the long bright years of the First Age, Man and Unicorn dwelt together, and both races grew in stature of body and mind.

On that very day when the Unicorn drew forth from the barren rock a gushing spring of life, the seeds of doom were sown as well. For even as those shining waters spread their fertile moisture, they poured into unlit fissures and trickled down to secret, burning caverns.

285

There, in those abysmal chambers, the sacred waters gave a life bestowing charge, first expended in the raising up of a living thing. And thus in the fire and the darkness was the Dragon. No other creature has possessed the same measure of strength and cunning.

The First Dragon is called Yaldabaoth, though she is known as Tiamat as well – and Yaldabaoth grew great and spawned others like herself. All dragons are then swift, sharp of intellect and thirst for knowledge.

While the Unicorn seeks to divine the secrets of creation that he may more perfectly know the Creative Source and share this knowledge with all of creation, the Dragon desires the same that is may hoard the knowledge and thereby gain dominance over the material realm, and in this way they believe they may conquer death, or rather...the Gates of Death.

Analyzing the ancient lore allows the seeker to understand the *Self* better. In contrast, the Formulae Draconis is none other than they very Dragonmind that has penetrated the psyche of man and for this, the race is no longer able to naturally maintain the spiritual balance necessary to actually remain 'spiritual-only' beings.

Naturally there is an inclination toward the possession of a 'physical vehicle' to experience the realm of form and a mind to act as the bridge of communication between the two. It is imperative, however, that this mind-channel remain clear to observe self-honest experience of reality.

CONDITIONS OF EXISTENCE

There are three conditions of existence which are to be, to do and to have.

The condition of being is the assuming of the identity of one's physical characteristics.

The condition of doing is the accomplishment of goals and the fulfillment of one's personal individualized purpose.

The condition of having is the ability to command or else take charge of the energy or space.

People assume identity programs that can get them attention whereas one is really giving their own energy into it and thereby can never enter the conditions of doing and having – therefore attaining no true power – they will simply *be*.

One who cannot attain their own satisfactory identity program will be quick to criticize that of others.

DETERMINATION

There are two types of determinism as applied to the current materials. An understanding of the first is a prerequisite to attainment of the second and it is indicated that humans are capable of both.

Self-Determinism is the personal power over the will to successfully accomplish a mission or task. This is self-mastery.

Pan-Determinism is the dictation of others. Once can dictate reality to another and it can be mutually agreed to through conscious acceptance or fought off as conscious rejection.

Being *Self-Determined* requires a strengthening of the will and conscious control of the mind for the *Self*. To extend this into the reality of others, in turn, requires the ability to consciously project an 'acceptable reality' into a group consciousness or "Group Mind."

SYSTEMOLOGY 101

The *alpha spirit* is in possession of a *human vehicle* that is manifold – containing a body, mind and spirit (or "Divine Spark"). Each co-exists with the others as one entity and yet the mind is able to see them as separate and manifold.

The *spirit* is not an 'object', an energy or a 'ball of light' as some magickal and esoteric traditions might have you believe. It is not manifest in form, thus not existent in the physical world or restricted to the physics of time and space as laws inhibit that which adheres to them. The *spirit* is the 'true creator' or Source – the *God in man* that displays all things in existence.

The *mind* is a communication center, which interprets one's environment via sensory stimuli and calculates the data that the body receives. The *Order of the Crystal Dawn* is most concerned with the *mind* as a focus. By better understanding the *mind* we might have a better avenue open to us in order that we might be able to later explore the *spirit* in true knowledge and *self-honesty*.

The analytical mind perceives the information

289

attained by the body, whereas the reactive mind utilizes and responds to this information via actions of the body. Clearly, the *body* is merely a physical storehouse – a vehicle – for the *mind* and *spirit* on the physical plane of existence as experienced by the body.

* * *

Whatsoever you seek or ask for, believe and speak as though you received it, and you shall receive it.

All creative thoughts – positive or negative that we can hold in our minds, that we can believe or fear, have a tendency to take form.

DREAMING

To obtain prophet dreams it is helpful to determine clearly in your mind precisely what you seek to discover. Observing the traditions of folk magic, you could make a 'dream pillow' using squares of purple fabric. Fill it with rosemary and lavender. You can also put a piece of small paper inside concerning what you seek to uncover in your dreams. Fold the piece of paper in half three times, put it in and sew it up.

If you seek to incorporate dreams or lucid dreaming as 'pathworking', you can 'incubate' your
dreams with an archetypal symbol, such as what
you find on most tarot cards. When you close
out the lights, continuing visualizing the symbols, filling your mind with the imagery as you
allow the subconscious to take over the sleep
phase.

Sometimes dreams are just dreams. And sometimes they are the subconscious mind trying to
let you know something significantly vital to a
current situation, or perhaps one that you are
about to face.

It is suggested in many "New Age" texts to
communicate with your 'spirit guides' and 'guardians' and even ask them to make appearances
and/or communicate with you in your dreams.

Those who have difficulty remembering their
dreams can use the affirmation, "I will awaken
remember my dream," prior to retiring.

Dreams can also be controlled – and certainly
there are many means of manipulating them, so
it is important not to overemphasize something
that is dreamed of when choosing or selecting a
course of physical action.

There is an ability for sorcerers and those in the Illuminati masquerading as 'aliens' to be able to enter and manipulate the dream world. It is an incredible feat to be able to reach a person in their sleep – but this is generally accomplished through the subconscious dreamscape.

Many complex methods involving astral work, remote viewing and the like can be employed, but there are also 'magickal' and 'ritual' forms of this experimental work as well. A key ingredient to this type of personalized magick is to be able to 'tap into' the 'energetic current' of the target – especially via imagery. Personal items and background information is excellent, but the photographic image (or even the ability to hold a similar clear image in the mind) is very important for success using these methods.

Outside the emergency uses of dream magick to warn of forthcoming doom, there are really only two purposes behind dream influence that we find reoccurring in magickal grimoires and mystic lore: making love to a person or bringing nightmares.

The most often found colors in these Illuminati based workings are red and black. Thus the Red Rite would be one that is focused on love and lust, whereas the Black Rite is used to torment. The color symbolism is saturated in the ritual space – candles, altar dressings, lighting, ritual attire, etc.

There is no specific verbiage or incantation that is necessary as this is purely an act of 'mental magick' and abilities – however, if you find that such is helpful for you to focus energy, then you can certainly write something simple for this.

Incense is helpful in this kind of working in order to focus the mind on a specific energy current – in this case, both are strengthened by scents that increase the perception of personal power. The Red Rite can be complimented with the fumes of jasmine and/or sandalwood. For the Black Rite, we recommend myrrh and/or dragon's blood – though sandalwood could be used for this one as well.

This type of working requires the raising of intense personal energy, emotional energy, in addition to incredible focus during release. Sex magick, usually in the form of masturbation, can also be used to aid in achieving these results.

TRANSCENDENCE

All things in physical existence have their own unique defining energetic signature or vibration that is experienced or interpreted on the physical plane. Humans also vibrate some kind of quality or nature – if we live in natural flow of universal forces, then the energy flow makes us satisfied individuals.

The nature of this transcendental property is the spark of Divine Consciousness which emenates from the Universal "Akasha" or spiritual essence of creation. From a material/physical paradigm or framework, a human is not programmed to experience this true nature of existence.

Deceptive illusions fill the space of the material world – glamours that lead to miseries, but understand that this physical existence is only temporary at best.

Every being has a true and eternal nature, its *alpha spirit*, that is connected or embodied of the essence of the 'fifth sphere' the realm of spiritual space that is outside of physical time-space perceptions of dimensional existence. The path of transcendence leads to perfect knowledge of the spheres – beginning with true self-knowledge.

The *herd* has no self-awareness, only the attachment to the 'group mind', and therefore exists only to meet the needs of the higher forms of life. Self-aware and capable beings value life, comprehend the problems and issues of existence in self-honesty and overcoming the mind-forged barriers of a physical existence.

Self-realization begins with *detachment* – the point when we realize that we are not these physical bodies that we have manifested for an outward existence – likewise, we are not the personality programs that we experience in forms manifested 'internally'. These are only physical and genetic vehicles for a material existence that is, in itself, fabricated solely for the purpose of the great ALL to experience itself.

If we can detach appropriately and elevate above the material physical limitations of this existence, then we can be freed also after death, and be able to understand the ways of the keepers of the *Gates of Death* – we will be able to transcend this sphere of existence when we die, rather than simply being reloaded into the *matrix* with recursive lessons.

When the body is not trained or programmed by

mind to perceive beyond what is deemed physical, it can easily become limited and trapped in its perceptions. Too often and too easily in modern times have people lost sight of their true purpose and so they begin to walk blindly, following in with the movement of the *herd*, seeking direction from those who are not even qualified to lead.

Of course, as soon as one sets out on the path of transcendence it is quite easy to be overwhelmed by the task and distracted by the many lights and colors of those who claim to shine on the way.

The true and singular voice of the Source of All speaks in a form that we are unable to hear when we are wrapped up in our material existence. As the philosopher of the East explains: In the Relative World the *knower* is the living spirit or superior energy and the *known* is the insignificant inferior energy.

THE RITE OF TRANSCENDENCE
(INSTALLATION OF A MASTER)

The "Rite of Transformation" is conducted in the ceremonial chamber of the lodge. The *master* is seated in the east. The *adept* stands in the west. The *deacon* (usually played by the candidate for *master*-to-be-installed) is positioned between the 'two pillars'.

The *priest* (assistant) stands at the south and acts as an aid to the *adept* for these proceedings. The *adept* acts as aid to the *master*. The *guard* is positioned at the door. Four 'elemental tablets' (whether *Enochian* or *Necronomical*) are placed at the four corners (quarters) of the ceremonial circle.

MASTER: The lodge is opened and the ceremony of the Transformation may now commence.

ADEPT: The Ceremony of Transformation may now commence.

DEACON: May I be allowed participation in the Rite of Transformation?

PRIEST: Guard, secure the entrance to this ceremonial lodge and seal the door.

The *guard* locks and seals the door.

PRIEST (to *Adept*): The ceremonial lodge is now sealed.

ADEPT (to *Master*): The ceremonial lodge is now sealed.

MASTER: With the lodge secure let us perform the Opening by Watchtower.

The *Opening by Watchtower* is performed.

[The Opening by Watchtower, also known as the Watchtower Formulae, is given in the *Sorcerer's Handbook of Merlyn Stone* as the "Watchtower Ceremony." Refer to that edition for performance instructions. -Ed.]

The ceremony continues.

ADEPT: In the name of *IAO*, I call forth the spirit of *n* to lay thy invisible hand upon our heads and bare witness to this, our solemn oath to the ascending light.

PRIEST: We call thee to aid and guard us in the name of and the glory of the *Tetragrammaton* – and by every unspeakable name of *God*.

MASTER: I call thee *secret brothers* in the spirit who are wise and merciful and who exist without end, for thy have no beginning in this realm. May we enter the abode and sanctuary of thy mysteries. Teach us, guide us, and descend thy gnosis upon us [especially *so-and-so* who is coming forth into mastery among us today.]

The *master* goes to the eastern tablet.

MASTER: By the ancient names and signs of the Creators, by the ancient spirit of Raphael and the Great King of the East, Bahtaheevah, behold and adore your creator. In the name of YHVH.

ADEPT: In and by the name IAO.

PRIEST: In and by the name Shahdye El Chye.

MASTER: I command that ye dwellers in the realm of the east, the kingdom of air, fashion for us the powerful foundation of Astral Light about us that we will be able to render our bodies transformed and approving to the Invis-ible Brotherhood.

The *deacon* (*master-to-be*) or *master* speaks the Third Enochian Key (given in the *Sorcerer's*

299

Handbook of Merlyn Stone).

MASTER: Etzarpeh.

ADEPT: Etzarpeh.

PRIEST: Etzarpeh.

DEACON: Etzarpeh.

MASTER: I invoke thee who are crossed by the stars and clad by the rays of the Sun. Thee who are the foundation of the universe. Look upon us and this ceremony and let your rays of power descend here to Awaken in our spirit the powers that shall prove a channel for thy Great Work. YHVH.

ADEPT: Yod-Heh-Vahv-Heh.

PRIEST: Yod-Heh-Vahv-Heh.

DEACON: Yod-Heh-Vahv-Heh.

MASTER: Shahdye el Chye.

ADEPT: Shahdye el Chye.

PRIEST: Shahdye el Chye.

DEACON: Shahdye el Chye.

MASTER: Great Spirit, grant to us thy presence.

ADEPT: By the spirits of the sphere of Yesod.

PRIEST: By the strength and power of Gabriel.

MASTER: O Great Ones of the sphere of Yesod, thee I do call here by the name of Shahdye El Chye and by the name of Gabriel, and the Great Ineffable Tetragrammaton, Yod-Heh-Vahv-Heh. May the powers of Yesod flow freely through here and prepare each of us [but especially *so-and-so* who is coming forth into mastery among us this day] for the way to the Great Work of Transcendence. IAO.

ADEPT: IAO

PRIEST: IAO

DEACON: IAO

MASTER: In the names and powers invoked this day I request the Radiance of Astral Light to descend upon us here and now which will transform our corruption to purity, which will

301

take out mortality and replace it with divinity of the Supernal Light with which comes greater health and vitality. In the strength of heart, mind and spirit, do we transfigure into the very embodiment of true magick and light in perfect knowledge. So mote it be.

ALL: So mote it be.

MASTER: Before all magickal manifestation comes the knowledge of the Light unending. Shemhamphorash.

ADEPT: Shemhamphorash.

PRIEST: Shemhamphorash.

DEACON: Shemhamphorash.

MASTER: In the name of the true spirit of creation and the universe – I dispel thee spirits who have been bound by this ceremony to return to thy place of dwelling but to come again when called. Depart with the blessings of this most holy Order.

ADEPT: Let the lodge be closed by the Rite of the Pentagrams.

The *deacon* is usually given permission to perform the closing *Lesser Banishing Ritual of the Pentagram* (given as the L.B.R.P. In the *Sorcerer's Handbook of Merlyn Stone*).

MASTER: I now declare the circle opened and this ceremony closed.

ADEPT: Guard, release the door.

MASTER: It is finished.

ALL: So mote it be.

ANTINOMIAN ENLIGHTENMENT

Previously we have spoken of the awakening and the illumination of the initiate. Now it is time to take the next step and approach the Master's *Ladder of Lights*.

Enlightenment is a manner of understanding through true knowledge or gnosis as opposed to worldly cognition. Gnosticism is a means of knowing via the inspiration in self-honesty of revelations of intuition – made possible by the integral merging of the *Self* with the *All*.

One common means of doing this is by way of a physical 'agent', one which is able to let us see free from herd assimilation. This is the main focus of the *Crystalline Sphere* discourse that was omitted from the current text.

To maintain control of the *Self* and inner worlds through self-administration of an 'agent' is a historically shamanic means to lower the veils that are perceived as "blockers" or "inhibitors" to seeing the reality of all-as-one.

In the world humans are subjected to on a daily basis – the modern ideals and values, systems of dependency for stability; are all inadequate and failing. Certainly, they have failed in assisting humans in maintaining their true knowledge of *Self*. Illuminated self-enlightenment requires that one stop depending on the world to dictate reality and the means for interpreting the reality.

In a world of depersonalization, we must demonstrate our own self-control and self-determination to regain the freedom of the spirit.

Cognitive and third-sphere methods of obtaining true knowledge fail us and yet society constitutes these as the more 'rational' avenues. This is what makes the wizard's world *occult*.

THE CRYSTALLINE SPHERE

This discourse is being prepared in conjunction with the treatise for the *Order of the Crystal Dawn*, titled Crystalline Awakening. It is the result of the experimentation of the *Elven Fellowship Circle of Magick* from 1998 to 1999 and may be omitted from the public presentations of the materials authored by *Merlyn Stone*.

This discourse is not representative of any of the systems previously disclosed by the *Elven Fellowship Circle of Magick* or the *Order of the Crystal Dawn* and should be archived for posterity purposes only. It should not be used in public as a representation of either organization until such a time when and if they have both disbanded.

At such a time, they may be disclosed, but for posterity only. Neither the authors or editors at any time in the course of the preparation of the various editions of this work condone or may be held responsible for its usage.

The authorship granted to this work is given as *Anonymous*, although the rights to it are to be held by the *Trust of Merlyn Stone*.

In the book I wrote for teens, *The Young Sorcerer*, I was, of course, seeking the approval of the parents and also not wanting to advocate anything illicit to minors when I said: "Drugs have no place in ceremony. Smoking is prohibited in most ritual." Naturally, I don't intend to go back on my words. It is true – in conventional magick, drugs really do have no place. It can therefore be clarified that this discourse is not on conventional magick – but rather unconventional magick – the magick of, let us say, the *Psychedelic Sorcerer.*

In conventional magick, the definition of the art is to "cause a change in external reality in accordance with one's internal will." In this methodology of "psychedelic magick" we can say that the definition of the art is to "cause an internal reality change regardless of external conditions – in accordance with one's will."

Anyone who has read my previous works is going to find this discourse a little bit outrageous. How can a 16 year old so eloquently talk on a topic so shocking? We will not speak of all the experiences and experiments that has made this work possible (though I am sure most of it will be omitted in later editions and the work is undoubtedly going to shrink as time goes on).

THREE TYPES OF PSYCHOACTIVE

<u>Sedatives</u> – decrease activity, induce calmness, produce rest and sleep.

<u>Stimulants</u> – increase activity, heighten alertness, enhance outward emotions.

<u>Psychedelics</u> – mind altering activity, perception alteration, thought and image enhancer.

CRYSTALLINE MAGICK

The four purposes or functions of 'crysalline magick' correspond to the four 'bodies' of a human being and also the four elements, etc. These concepts were derived from the section "Planning a Session" in Timothy Leary's classic text, *Psychedelic Experience*. Purpose number one is intellectual – of the mind, number two is physical – involving others in the world, three is emotional and the fourth is spiritual.

1. For increased personal power, intellecutal understanding, sharpened insight into self and cultural improvement of the life situation, accelerated learning and professional growth.

307

2. For duty, helping of others, providing care, rehabilitation, rebirth of fellow men.

3. For fun, sensuous enjoyment, aesthetic pleasure, interpersonal closeness and the experience of it.

4. For transcendence, liberation from the ego and space-time limitations, attainment of mystical union.

Thus, it is suggested that mind, body, emotion and spirit can all be unlocked through the use of 'crystalline magick'.

* * *

Ask any ex-EFCOM member about "Item #3" and they will probably giggle. In the *Elven Fellowship Circle of Magick* (which disbanded just prior to the full establishment of the *Order of the Crystal Dawn*), "Item #3" was cannabis.

The outline of the coven meetings became as follows:

Item #1 – Ritual
Item #2 – Training and Lessons
Item #3 – Cannabis

Eventually, #1 and #2 were integrated with #3.

ENOCHIAN AETHYRS ON ACID

Depending on the potency, a practitioner may take anywhere from 2 to 4 *hits* of acid (LSD). Varying with the dosage and method of administration, it can take between 30 and 60 minutes to begin to take effect. This gives you ample time to set up the environment and perform the Opening by Watchtower (ceremony) and the Call to the Aethyrs [all of which is provided in the *Sorcerer's Handbook of Merlyn Stone*].

Sit in the center of your circle (nemeton) and wait for the acid (LSD) to take effect. Once this occurs, stand and face the appropriate direction of the aethyr you wish to access, reciting the appropriate calls and being sure to invoke the necessary guardians (governors) from the Body of Light. Don't forget your L.B.R.P.

MERLYN'S NECRONOMICON

In addition to the *Sorcerer's Handbook*, the other *Merlyn Stone* discourse to receive critical public attention was the final volume released, titled: *Necronomicon*.

The *Necronomicon of Merlyn Stone* should not be confused with the section of the *Sorcerer's Handbook* that was dedicated to the "Simon" *Necronomicon*. However, both that section and the separate *Necronomicon* discourse were later critically reviewed in *The Necronomicon Files* by Daniel Harms and John Gonce.

This discourse is by no means a replacement for the study of the *Necronomicon*, particularly the serious subject of the modern faction of *Mardukite Chamberlains* – but at the time of preparing this discourse, the people I was working with, *The Order of the Crystal Dawn* were in want of a "Necronomicon." And so the work was prepared using the materials that had not made their way into *The Sorcerer's Handbook* or *Crystalline Awakening*, thereby completing what had been first outlined by the *Elven Fellowship Circle of Magick* as the "Sorcerer's Trilogy."

311

The "Introduction" written for this work, which was intended as an in-house production only with no intent of seeing public surfacing, in addition to using the title "Necronomicon" actually sparked significant controversy outside the *Crystal Dawn* once the materials did surface.

THE NECRONOMICON
An Introduction

Many myths, tales and texts have been put into print and hinted at in the occult underground, fantasy bookshelves and in Hollywood, but what is the *Necronomicon* really?

The *Necronomicon* is merely an archetype – a symbol – one that is seemingly universal to all humans: the concept of the 'sacred book', one which will reveal the secrets of the "unknown" to those selective few privileged ever to possess it.

Consequently, as the story goes, there is only one book in circulation – one true copy – which would obviously make it a rare find. For the life of the beholder, no one else would be able to possess the same power and knowledge.

...and it is unlikely that the beholder would simply *give* the book away – though they might be killed for it, or somehow *by* it.

The *Necronomicon mythos* often hints at an underground 'cabal' of "those who know." It is possible that the origins of the *Necronomicon* are also the origins of the mysterious factions of "ceremonial high magick" as it is known in the Western World.

A book prescribed to be the *Necronomicon* would then hold within it the very foundations of "ceremonial magick" in its purest form and would then be passed down from the mysterious 'givers of knowledge' to the egyptians, greeks, druids, kabbalists, alchemists, cathars, templars, rosicrucians, masons, the golden dawn and now the modern contemporary "New Age" movement...

Teach those who show an open mind and the potential for the *occult*. Shall every master of the *occult* take on one apprentice in their lifetime to be their successor. And if that one proves wrong, choose another. Choose only the best among them, and then, only when the time is right to pass on the mysteries.

* * *

Creativity swept over my original writing of the work for the *Crystal Dawn*, which was made up of primarily young adults who enjoyed the symbolism and archetypal usage of obscure books and methods in their practices. The preface for the work alluded to several open-ended claims or citations that were meant to give the book some solidity, though it was really a compendium of ceremonial magick.

* * *

USING THIS BOOK

This book is definitely not *orthodox*, though it is an intriguing grimoire of the magickal arts. It is not set up in any certain manner or sequence, nor is it even catalogued by tables or indexes. Such is all the better for grimoires and notebooks such as the *Necronomicon*.

The *Necronomicon* changes in time and space as there is always room for additions made by the beholder during their lifetime – as such no two people truly read the same *Necronomicon* in the same 'light' as each goes into its forbidden pages seeking for their own private motives and desires. All wish to know what they want to know.

Carbon dating on the original book shows its existence in times c. 6,000 B.C.E., though we can really not be sure. Nothing within the *Necronomicon* is dated either.

There is really no set *mythos* for the *Necronomicon*, as the pantheons have changed with each new culture's ambassador making their own contributions to the legacy. The most well known of these is attributed to the *Sumerians* and *Babylonians*, which were the original holders or creators of the book...

...good luck from the *Crystal Dawn*.

...we hope you find what you're searching for.

A GRIMOIRE OF MACHT

After the completion of the *Necronomicon of Merlyn Stone*, the *Order of the Crystal Dawn* decided against the further public distribution of the materials and so the perceived legacy of *Merlyn Stone*, in essence, disappeared. The members that remained after 1999 enjoyed the writings that I was producing enough to continue contibuting to the private printing costs of circulating small print runs of materials. Even the *Necronomicon of Merlyn Stone* only saw a small printing of 50 copies whereas the *Sorcerer's Handbook* has seen thousands.

The *Grimoire of Macht* was a codename given to what had already been compiled for the *Crystal Dawn* under other titled such as *Gatherum* or *Myrlynomicon*. It was nothing short of an early attempt at *Arcanum*, seeking to solidify all of the composite *Merlyn Stone* materials into one volume. These editions were restricted to members of the *Order* only and never saw the same distribution as other *Merlyn Stone* books. The public release of *Crystalline Awakening* and the *Necronomicon* showed we were reaching limitations in our self-publishing methods and also our means of distribution.

What the work I did for these smaller groups allowed for was the perfection of my own skills in book design and writing for the occult base. I was not yet ready to come into my own for the sake of the *Mardukites* and so I was still in a position to 'practice' so to speak. And those who were involved with me enjoyed what I was doing significantly. Rising printing and distribution costs merely caused us to have to resign from public attention and finally in 2001, I had realized that I had reached my own limits from what I had already been exposed to and so I retired into the underground for nearly a decade before resuming my position as *Nabu* in 2008 with the founding of *Mardukite Ministries*.

The writing style and premise for the collected *Grimoire of Macht* is significantly more representative of the candid first-hand language base I have found I still tend to resort to.

* * *

Here do I therefore gather together the ancient magick into this sacred book. I collect it for posterity – for the future generations, that the mysteries shall not be lost due to any blind folly.

This book contains the power to change the world and know too that the powers released shall ever change the beholder. Magick – true magick – opens eyes; and one opened, you cannot look away.

Perhaps my deed is done by constucting this tome – I was not allowed the use of it all, but enough to satisfy by own life and will. My own unique variations have been used by those whom my works have met, and may the gods look favorably on them.

This magick which drives my pen is of such an intensity that no step should be overlooked, no detail dismissed unless thou be qualified to properly alter these works – but do not copy or distribute this work, unless it be in its entirety.

In return for the manifestation of this compend-ium, I ask only that my wishes be met and you have been warned. For my powers grow, even in death, for I am now infinite.

If you use any charm, spell, incantation or breathe out loud any passage henceforth, you put yourself at the mercy of the pact known to the ancient brotherhood. If you stand against this code – if you go against the forces of the universe – there shall be no mercy for you.

Reveal not the presence of this book to any while it is in your possession. No one, except during that time in thou life when before thy death, when it will be of no more use to you, can it then be passed to them who it will best serve – and who will serve it best.

Under no circumstances shall this book be sold. And for each cent in profit thou makes, may you be a thousand times cursed by the *Ancient Ones*. Do not thou test me! I offer you the world but can just as easily take it away again.

If you use this sorcery, keep clear intention, and harm none whom do not wish you ill, or I shall render you powerless. For I have walked among the *ancient spirits* that you now call and I am no stranger to their ways. I can cut you off – and I will if necessary.

And if thou rejects your path, charge another to go in your place, lest I send hordes of angry spirits to attack and torment thee. There must always be *one* to hold the *key* to the mysteries.

Do not keep this book on shelves where the idle stares of others will capture it – nor should it come into contact with any other book at all. It must be kept separate – secret – in a hidden place. Speak of it not – nor should you alter your life in such ways that society will suspect you have something hidden.

As the ink runs from this pen so shall I run you down ye dismiss my words. And if thou tear any part of this book, may the lords of the pit tear away your breath of life.

You know not I, but I am watching you. There are those in the Hebrew tongue who call me *Nebo* or by my given name in this life Yehshuah which you know also as Jesus, others know me as *Nabu*, or *Merlyn* and those who know me, know me as a prodigy of the mystical arts.

I have traversed the spheres where the *spirits* dwell, so too have I seen *God* and *lived*. The Great Mysteries of the All-as-One will be revealed to thee when thou art ready.

Fear not these powers within, lest they render thee as their slave. Master the magick within yourself and take these secrets as thy own.

Substitute nothing, except which is acceptable, and you will know.

Do not shortcut the magick or show ill reverence to the true power. For if you abuse this power it will discard thee as a weed from a flower bed.

As to me, my spirit may be called in the dense forests and woodlands that men seldom travel or steal the innocence from with their gaze, or in patches of trees found within long flat plains and fields. I am drawn to the flame quenched with fire – to the smoke that travels through the air carrying my spirit. If you silence yourself in these places, my voice can be heard.

Forget not my true name – that I will hear it and remember. In my guise as the *Merlyn*, my colors are purple and green and my number is nine. But in my more ancient form of *Nabu*, my color is blue and my numbers are 12, 6 and 2...

TRUTH AGAINST THE WORLD

Written in 1997 to be broken up in parts for a "Knowledge Lecture" series that was originally prepared for the *Draconis Celtic Lodge of Druids* but was later adopted into the archives of the *Elven Fellowship Circle of Magick*. A sum-mary version was later used in place of other more questionable materials in the 2005 release of *Merlyn's Magick*.

* * *

THE PERSONAL QUEST FOR TRUTH

Truth is the essence of life. Trust is the unseen power that governs all things. Truth is the key to unlocking the secrets of the universe. But in the material realm, truth becomes subjective in experience as no two people appear to share the same 'truth'. It is through the understanding of our 'personal truth' that we might better understand the nature of ourselves and why we think, feel and act the way we do.

It is written that if you try to understand the unvierse, you will discover nothing at all, but seek to understand the *self* and there alone lies the Great Key to the mysteries of all creation.

KNOW THYSELF

Socrates said many times to know thyself – and those two simple words have meaning of utmost imporance here. What he meant was that by understanding human nature, all else that could be desired to know, would fall into place.

What many *Druids* today do not grasp is that before one seeks to know about trees, rocks, animals and otherworlds, that they should first come to know themselves. Humans are like a collage of what could be labelled mind, body and spirit, which are simultaneously connected and separate – not altogether different than the 'mystery' of the "Holy Trinity" in Catholicism.

SCIENCE vs. SPIRIT

Contemporary systems of science do not really understand the multifaceted aspects of humans because science is only programmed with the ability to establish physical and mundane basis for phenomenon and existence. For science, man is only a brain; the 'mind' is nonexistent.

The brain is programmed to be a construct limited to the physical reality of existence. The mind, on the contrary, is not a physical form and is full of unlimited potentiality. It is through Truth that we are able to unlock the unlimited power of the mind.

AGELESS TRUTH

One issue with the quest for the Truth is that the ability to perceive it clearly and the thirst for the quest can be lost with age.

INEFFABLE TRUTH

I must point out here the semantic difference between "Truth" and "truth." There are "truths" all around us – but they are composed by man, built upon the language structure and definitions entangled together to provide arbitrary meanings.

In youth, a child has yet to be conformed to this semantic level of 'truth' and it is at this point that they might be unconditionally brought to recognize reality self-honestly for the remainder of their life.

PERFECT BALANCE

The path to the Truth is not necessarily one that is focused on 'perfect balance' of forces in the material world – in fact, on a physical level this idea of perfect balance can never be attained.

A *druidic doctrine* exists that explains that the human spirit needs a 'constructive imbalance' to grow, whereas true 'balance' is actually 'static' and promotes stagnation of energy.

When the time comes for you to be 'perfectly balanced' you will not be able, or have need to, exist in the physical world, which is everything but static and unchanging. All manifestation is in some state of 'imperfection' on a 'spiritual' "level."

SEMANTIC ISSUES ON THE QUEST

One step often missed on the quest for truth is that one is even forced to analyze what "Truth" means. How can you know you have found the Truth if you don't know what it is? Likewise, how can you quest for something you don't know? We must determine what is true and how we can know it to be true.

Can we turn to a man-made knowledge to distinguish the truth? No, because it is the man-made truths that limit us in our programming and place barriers on what we are capable of understanding socially.

SEEK AND YE SHALL FIND

Many believe that knowledge can only be gained through direct physical and personal experiences – but we also know that this is not the case.

It is said that Truth can be found in the unity of 'experiencing, studying and knowing' all things, but the Truth may not be found in any *one* of those three things.

Truth may be gained or at least brought closer to your reach through what Socrates called "Right Action" and philosophers and mystics often refer to as the "Right Way." This is living in accordance with the natural forces of the universe and by one's true and self-honest intuition.

"Men have always gone to their graves preaching their own truths; yet the sun still rises."

We must understand that "beliefs" will come and go, religions will open and shut, civilizations will rise and fall but the ineffable Truth of All Thing will remain unchanged.

SOCIAL PROGRAMMING

Holding on to tightly to man-made truths will cancel out what is real because this type of artificial truth programming seeks immediate dominance, but will fade, leaving its believer in "darkness" trying to grasp on whatever will hold them. Another man-made truth program will be there to replace the first and so on.

RITUALISM

Many interpret the search for truth, or this type of philosophy or *Druidry* as a magick – and in many ways it is depending on your semantics, but the 'practical magick' and ritualism is merely an 'outward' expression of the 'inner' search for "Truth," or at least they *should* be.

So, in order to gain a 'peaceful' environment we must radiate peace from within – like attracts like.

THE TRI-FORCE

The methodology of questing for truth and the 'tri-force' is also existence in a fiction based *Order* called the *Delta Knights* – which sought the Truth in Knowledge comprised of Strength, Wisdom and Compassion.

To attempt to reach the Truth while on the physical plane is to stand on a ladder delicately balanced and composed of many far-reaching aspects. Skip one step, and you fall backwards. Misinterpret your foundation, and your ladder will not balance. Seek the false truths, and your ladder will be left leaning against the sky with nothing of substance to hold it upright.

...and when the student is ready,
the teacher shall appear.

THE SORCERER'S NOTEBOOK

With compilation beginning in 1998, the *Sorcerer's Notebook* was a large leather compendium kept by the *Elven Fellowship Circle of Magick* and was the precursor for the infamous *Sorcerer's Handbook*. Much of the latter volume was extracted from this work, although several portions were not, which can now be included here.

* * *

CRYSTAL POWER

The Atlantean Power Rod is constructed from a hollow copper pipe tube with a copper cap at one end. The quartz crystal is placed at the other end as should be 1 1/2 to 3 inches long.

The outer surface of the tube-rod should be wrapped in leather. Combat rods are wrapped in black; healing rods are traditionally blue, red and green – but really any color will work for a multipurpose rod.

The crystal rod is used to direct currents of energy through visualization. Healing rods may have crystals at both ends.

The Atlantean Crystal Headband helps to amp-
lify psychic/psionic powers. Take a sheet of thin
copper, cut an bend to form a band. A silver disc
or coin about two inches in diameter is fastened
to the front of the band. A quartz with a flat end
is then affixed to the disc. You may wish to
punch holes at the far ends of the copper to
attach some leather so it can be tied around your
head.

FROM THE GRAND GRIMOIRE

To make the spirits of three young ladies appear
in the Sorcerer's room, eat no meat or fatty
foods for three days. On the fourth day, clean
your bedroom and fast for the entire day. Be
that sure no one else enters the room on that
day. Have nothing on the walls and freshly
washed white linen on the bed.

After dinner, go to the room and light a good
fire (or you can use many candles). Set up a
table with a clean white tablecloth and three
chairs. Have a loaf of white bread and a glass of
water at each setting. Then put a chair beside
your bed.

Once in bed, recite the following:

Besticitum consolatio veni ad me vertat creon creon creon cantor laudem omnipotentis et non commentur. Stat superior carta blent lauden omviestra principiem da montem et inimicos meos o prostrantis vobis et mihi dantes que passium fieri sincisibus.

The spell will last until midnight, at which time the three will depart. And the sorcerer should the window open so they may enter.

MENTAL EARPHONE

Thoughts need not be spoken to be heard. Sounds can be sent out in subvocalizations, subtle vibrations of the throat and also mentally. Sounds can be produced from the mind and transmit through the air. You can even listen to your own thoughts!

To hear the thoughts of others you must practice deep relaxation. Keep the mind free and connect to the person based on what you know of them and the energetic connection. When you are attuned, relax and allow thoughts to come.

FREEWILL PROGRAM

Although humans possess a 'freewill program', it is still a program within a system – and there are conceivably 'external' factors which are the influences of life forming the 'program'.

There are the experiences we take on of our *alpha spirits* – and those connected to *past lives* of that *spirit*. There are also karmic agreements proposed prior to this incarnation that play an important part in our program.

The *genetic vehicle* and our heredity make up the physical body that is used to interact with the physical realm.

Factors such as these will undoubtedly contribute to the way in which 'reality' is experienced. And those experiences will also be subject to the program we follow, feeding that program by conforming to our beliefs and previous knowledge and experience.

Thus, the natural state of the human is as a *free spirit*, but with the responsibility of occupying a physical body comes the necessity to deal with its many programmed influences.

NECRONOMICON GNOSIS

Necronomicon Gnosis is a fragmentary note-book that was never actually compiled into a book in itself, but readers of the *Merlyn Stone* chronicles, or more specifically, the modern *Mardukite* works by Joshua Free, will notice the basis of many of the more recent studies, comparisons and experiments from this work.

* * *

Primary elements involved: water and air. The heights, depths and "spaces between."

"Cthulhu" -> "Tutulu" (Tutu-lu); a name appearing in *Liber 418*, Crowley's Book of the Zonei (Aires).

Zootypes of the Gods, as non-human beasts, a reference to taboo hybrid intercourse between types of beings; humans and animals – or gods and humans.

1955-1962 O.T.O. New Isis Lodge established; communication between the O.T.O. and the *Sumerian* "Old Ones" begins.

| Lovecraftian: | Depths (Cthulhu) |
| | Heights (Yog-Sothoth) |

MaKaShaNa:	Ma – Maat (space)
	Ka – Kali (water/blood)
	Sha – Shiva/Set (fire/spirit)
	NA – Niggurath (earth/ matter)

Necronomicon Gnosis –

The power of man is the power of the Ancient Ones.

The Formula of 0=2 –

Not two parts synthesized to produce a third.
 - not 1+1 = 2
 - not -1 +1 = 0
Negation of a non-negative
and a non-positive.
 - absolute negation.
 - no duality.

YEZIDI

The Yezidi are a Mesopotamian sect still in existence in northern Iraq. They have a unique culture and genetics. They speak of a 'god of the black mountain' and refer to a "Black Book" and a 'peacock angel' – some obscure facets...

"Melek Ta'us" – "Yazdan"

Significance of 360; with 360 lamps.

Name "Shaitan" not spoken but revered as 'exalted one' or 'chief prince'.

Yezidi claim to be of Adamic descent but not from Eve – suggestive that the outside world is of a different genetics.

VISIONS & VOICE

Hermetic Order of the Golden Dawn, MacGregor Mathers, Crowley and the "Secret Chiefs" or "Invisible Brotherhood" that led or influenced the elite of the order.

MAAT – the "true word" (truth)
Power in truth. Power in the word.

The Sound. Silence.
The Voice. The Word.
Vibration. Sound...

* * *

Order of the "Dark Crystal" = IXAXAAR
Death Cult = Gate Cult
Cross = Crossing

CROSSING TO THE ABYSS

1. Surrendering Self to the *spirit of the white mound* or the *spirit of the hill*, tower, etc. (sem.)

2. Slaying of all thoughtforms. Indicative of the 'slaying of the dragon' – the dragonmind, etc.

* * *

The Ego is reinforced
to keep out the voice of the stars.

* * *

Mystical experience – subject with absence of object.
Magickal experience – object with absence of subject.

338

Divine Spark (1)
 Supernal Trinity (3)
  Governors of the Spheres (7)
    Seats of the Zodiacal Wheel (12)

Zodiacal age = 2,160 years.
1 degree = 72 years.

Taurian age → Aryan age → Piscean Age

EFCOM BOOK OF SHADOWS

Compiled in 1998, the *Book of Shadows* belonging to the *Elven Fellowship Circle of Magick* was edited by "*Merlyn Stone*" and released in its entirety as the "Second Edition" of the *Sorcerer's Handbook* exclusively to members of EFCOM. The text was far removed from what the public knew as the *Sorcerer's Handbook of Merlyn Stone* and consisted only of rituals and magickal operations without background instruction, which was provided to members of EFCOM first hand.

Various passages, ritual texts and operations have been excerpted from the *EFCOM Book of Shadows* in the past, including the 2005 edition of *Merlyn's Magick*, the *Arcanum* work of Joshua Free and *Book of Elven-Faerie*. Portions of the work not previously excerpted may now be reprinted here for posterity.

RITE OF THE BLADE

Before the energies of the circle have been raised, each *DruWitch* undergoes a quick but meaningful initiation into the circle.

The East *DruWitch* (or leader) stands at the eastern zone of the circle's boundaries and the members are lined up (elementally) clockwise, behind the South *DruWitch*.

The East *DruWitch* holds the black-handled dagger with his right hand to the left breast of the South *DruWitch*. His left hand is on the South *DruWitch*'s right shoulder. The ritual proceeds in a manner similar to what is seen in the motion picture: *The Craft*.

EAST: It would be better for you to rush upon this blade then to enter our circle with fear in your heart. How do you enter?

SOUTH: With perfect love and perfect trust.

EAST: I welcome you to the circle as a 'free person' (handing off the dagger to the South *DruWitch*).

SOUTH (to WEST): It would be better for you to rush upon this blade then to enter our circle with fear in your heart. How do you enter?

WEST: With perfect love and perfect trust.

SOUTH: I welcome you to the circle as a 'free

person' (handing off the dagger to the West *DruWitch*).

WEST (to NORTH): It would be better for you to rush upon this blade then to enter our circle with fear in your heart. How do you enter?

NORTH: With perfect love and perfect trust.

WEST: I welcome you to the circle as a 'free person' (handing off the dagger to the North *DruWitch*).

The *North DruWitch* hands the dagger to the leader or continues initiating other members of the circle. When this has been completed, the leader then begins the *Casting of the Circle*.

CASTING THE CIRCLE

Members enter from the *east* and take their places around the circle.

EAST: We consecrate this circle to the power of *Menw* and *Awen*.

SOUTH: May they hear our calls and bless us with power.

WEST: May the *Ancient Ones* and *Elder Gods* aid and protect our sacred ring.

NORTH: We stand at a threshold between worlds in a veil of mystery.

EAST: ORO IBAH AOZPI – in the names and letters of the great eastern quadrangle, I invoke thee spirits of the watchtower of the east.

SOUTH: OIP TEAA PDOKE – in the names and letters of the great southern quadrangle, I invoke thee spirits of the watchtower of the south.

WEST: MPH ARSL GAIOL – in the names and letters of the great western quadrangle, I invoke thee spirits of the watchtower of the west.

NORTH: MOR DIAL HKTGA – in the names and letters of the great northern quadrangle, I invoke thee spirits of the watchtower of the north.

EAST: May the powers of the watchtower guardians be ever with us.

NORTH: May the powers of Menw and Awen ever be with us.

344

SOUTH: Let us conjure the powers of the masters to be with us.

WEST: And may with their powers come the wisdom to use it.

EAST: From the eastern city of Gorias, I summon master Esras. Bring the mighty Spear of Lugh and stand as guardian in the east.

SOUTH: From the southern city of Finias, I summon master Uscias. Bring the Sword of Nuada and stand as guardian in the south.

WEST: From the western city of Murias, I summon master Semias. Bring the Cauldron of the Dagda and stand as guardian in the west.

NORTH: From the northern city of Falias, I summon master Morfessa. Bring the Stone of Fal and stand as guardian in the north.

EAST: May the energies of the four masters gather here.

The ritual nemeton has now been consecrated for magickal work by the coven.

DISSOLUTION OF THE CIRCLE

The circle must be ceremonially 'opened' or 'distinguished' if the powers have been called to 'close' or 'cast' it.

Stand at the center of the nemeton (circle) and say:

As I have come to this circle in love and fellowship, so do I leave in the same way. May I spread the peace and love that I have known here outwardly to the world.

Raise your arms, saluting the powers, saying:

I now ask the elemental forces called here to return to their duties in Nature. I thank them for their attendance and for watching of me (us) and this sacred circle during the rites of magick. Lords and Ladies of the elves, sylphs, and creatures of faerie – my thanks and blessings go with you for sharing this time with me.

Meditate in the center of the circle, focusing on the higher powers that have been called to your circle. Face north, dismissing them, saying:

Now, the magick work is done, the mystic web

has been woven of mortal mind, heart and soul. Helpful to they who choose to follow the ways of the mighty spirits of our ancestors – baneful to those who choose to oppose the Elder Gods, the ancient and shinning ones.

Move counter-clockwise around the circle, dismissing each of the individual powers that were called specifically in the 'casting of the circle' or other preliminary operations. Ground out any superfluous energies, then use the dagger to split the circle, saying:

The circle is open but never broken.

LOVE-SPELL CEREMONY

This ceremony was written for solitary use by members of the *Elven Fellowship Circle of Magick*, though it has also been adapted for group usage. It is based on diverse workings of a similar nature and has been used and modified effectively numerous times by various folks.

This spell is to be practiced for seven days in succession, preferably during the waxing cycle of the moon and beginning on a Friday. Each day the two candles representative of the couple are to be moved closer together until they nearly touch. A variation of this working has also been used for 'separation' magick, to sever the energies of a couple, whereby the candles are brought away from each other each day, and the working begins on a saturday.

The *circle is cast* and the *DruWitch* says:

O mighty Menw and Awen, hear my plea to you; my plea of love for ___ and his/her desire.

Call down the powers of personal assistants in magick, co-magicians, the quarters and the masters. Then say:

I ___ being armed with power by the Supreme Majesty, by Menw and Awen, I do strongly command that by the powerful princes, ministers and the Chief Prince, by the four masters, Esras, Uscias, Semias and Morfessa, that I do bind ___ to love me in accordance with my will.

By the powers of Menw and Awen, and by the arcane forces of EL, Adonai, Elohi, Ehih Asar Ehih, Tzabaoth, IAO, Elyon, IA, Shaddai el Chye and by the ineffable name of the Tetragrammaton, YHVH, that I bind ___ to love me with peace and no difficulty or harm to anyone.

An "Abramelin square" may be employed here, or you can simply speak the (first five) names:

Sator, Arepo, Tenet, Opera, Rotas. Iah. Iah. Iah. Enam. Iah. Iah. Iah. Be ye the powers around me, at mine aid, for that which I desire.

Transfer to the powers invoked to the *Self* and light the candle representative of *Self* (on the right side of the altar – projective side), saying:

This is myself and the flame burns as does my spirit. The love I have for ____ is great and burns deep within my being.

Transfer the energies raised to the 'other person' and light the candle representative of them (on the left side – receptive side), saying:

The is the heart and soul of ____, whom I see and picture before me.

Visualize the person in your mind's eye coming toward you, thinking of you, etc. Light the foundation candle, in the middle closest to you and between the two sections/divisions of the altar, saying:

The love ____ has for me grows with this flame.

349

It burns as does this candle as forever drawn to me. Great is the love ___ has for me. Great is the love I have for ___ .

Visualize the couple embracing as the crown candle is lit, in the middle farthest from you, saying:

By the powers of Menw and Awen, I draw him/ her to me – the one toward the other. Powerful is my persuasion. The thought of me shall be constant.

See the person clearly – or the couple embracing together. Send energy to the vision and say:

My spell is upon you O' ___ , as my desire for you is great. My spell is upon you ___ , may love blossom and sweeten between us (them). My spell is upon you ___ , I have directed the powers of the universe to coax you into my arms.

Release all energy raised toward the goal and ground any superfluous energies of the nemeton. Thank and dismiss all powers called and extinguish (open) the circle.

THE GREAT TREE RITE

The *Great Tree Rite* is based on a text from the *Draconis Celtic Lodge of Druids* baring the same name. The version included here, used by the *Elven Fellowship Circle of Magick* is the third revision (1998).

The *Great Tree* is the major 'sacred tree' that the coven (and its individuals) use the most for their magickal work, group meetings, healing and possibly oracular use. This rite is practiced on the *new moon* of each month.

LEADER: We are here to give witness to the unity of the circle, represented by the sacred tree, our symbol of love – the love we share. We are the children of the light at one with the great tree. You, sacred tree are the embodiment of our circle, the symbol of our progression through this existence and through the sacred earth year.

NORTH: Its beginnings, middles and ends.

EAST: Its balance and equality.

WEST: And there must be times of celebration and festivities.

SOUTH: Here we celebrate the strength of the circle. May we, the guardians of the earth and its elements, aid in honoring the great tree.

EAST: I offer a season of growth as the sun greets the spring.

SOUTH: I offer a season of fullness as the sun warms the summer.

WEST: I offer a season of change with the tides of autumn.

NORTH: I offer a time of knowing the inner self as the earth hibernates in winter.

LEADER: The roots of this sacred tree shall stretch, extending deep within our being, offering nourishment and stability to its faithful guardians.

EAST: And in between the roots and branches we shall stand as its guardians, Druids who are imitators of the Oak.

SOUTH: The strength of the sun – the *Sky Father* – is within us. We shall reflect the pattern of the *Great Tree* in our spiritual growth.

WEST: In the expression of our guardianship, the reflected image of the *Great Tree* will radiate from us, always.

NORTH: May we grow together as the trees in the forest, each beautiful in its own way, our roots reaching into the same rich earth.

EAST: Out branches reaching into the same bright sky.

WEST: May we grow to our full potential, into beauty from the seeds we now are.

SOUTH: O' spirit of the *Great Tree*, we are your worthy guardians.

ALL: Spirit of the *Great Tree*, we are your worthy guardians.

LEADER: We are united in our strength and faith, yet we can delight in our differences. Forever shall you be within us, *Great Tree!*

As this ceremony does not require the formal consecration of a circle, the powers need not be dismissed (and the circle extinguished) if they were not called forth for the preliminaries of the operation.

CALLING THE POWERS
(ALTERNATE)

EAST: Now we do breathe; not only air, but the very breath of magick.

SOUTH: Closed may the circle be, under the protection of the *Tetragrammaton*.

WEST: May the powers 'above' and 'below' come forth to help and guide this work.

NORTH: We stand at a threshold between worlds, in a veil of mystery.

EAST: ORO IBAH AOZPI *Shemhamphorash.*

ALL: *Shemhamphorash.*

SOUTH: OIP TEAA PDOKE *Shemhamphorash.*

ALL: *Shemhamphorash.*

WEST: MPH ARSL GAIOL *Shemhamphorash.*

ALL: *Shemhamphorash.*

NORTH: MOR DIAL HKTGA *Shemhamphorash.*

ALL: *Shemhamphorash.*

EAST: By draconian power, may this circle be sealed.

SOUTH: Dragons of spirit, bless this circle with your fire.

WEST: Behold – we await the power and guidance of the *Dragon's Breath.*

NORTH: From *Grail*, ruler of the earth, does power come.

EAST: From *Sarys*, ruler of the air, does power come.

SOUTH: From *Fafnyr*, ruler of the fire, does power come.

WEST: From *Nalyon*, ruler of the water, does power come.

NORTH: Dragons of *Destruction* and *Choas*, be here now to extinguish and destroy all the evil forthcoming.

EAST: In the names of *Menw* and *Awen*, rulers of the earth, lords of the realm, we request the

355

forces of your power to be with us now.

SOUTH: Open wide the gates of your power and come forth from the *Abyss* to greet us as your allies and co-magicians in a realm of magick and power.

WEST: Come forth and be one with us; we take thy names as our own that you will favor us who honor thee.

NORTH: Answer to thy names by manifesting our desires this day/night...

A ceremonial rite or act of spellcraft may now be conducted within the nemeton.

AN ELVEN DRUID'S CURSE

To curse another obtain an *oak leaf* and *four black candles*. The oak leaf will come to symbolize your enemy and the four candles are to surround it at each 'direction'. It is best if the candle has their name written on it in charcoal (or you can burn the end of a stick and write with it).

Then intone:

Behold, saith me – the mighty voices of my vengeance smash the stillness of the air and I am a master of annihilation. May the powers of the four fighters –

Esras (light east candle),
Uscias (light south candle),
Semius (light west candle)
and Morfessa (light north candle),

– come and fix this curse upon thee, o' ___ who has caused me me anguish.

Light the leaf on fire and visualize your enemy burning.

INITIATION #3

The *initiate* stands in the center of a conjured circle. The members of the *Inner Circle* are present. The *Outer Circle* is not allowed to take part or witness.

LEADER: You come into the *inner circle* in the illumination of *Awen*. Repeat: The illumination of *Awen* / the illumination of seasons / the illumination of the elements / the illumination of days and nights / may *Awen's* light / kindle in the heart and head of all / and may light be lifted unto *Menw*.

EAST: You enter the *inner circle* in the light of clear vision. Will you strive to uphold the element of air?

INITIATE: I shall.

EAST: Then breathe deeply the purity of air.

The *initiate* is littered with rose petals.

SOUTH: You enter the *inner circle* in the light of clear purpose. Will you strive to uphold the element of fire?

INITIATE: I shall.

SOUTH: Then breathe deeply the strength of fire.

The *initiate* is 'fumed' with *dragon's blood* incense smoke.

WEST: You enter the *inner circle* in the light of clear wisdom. Will you strive to uphold the element of water?

INITIATE: I shall.

WEST: Then breathe deeply the tides of clear water.

The *initiate* is sprinkled with blessed waters.

NORTH: You enter the *inner circle* in the light of clear faith. Will you strive to uphold the element of earth?

INITIATE: I shall.

NORTH: Then breathe deeply the roots of the earth.

The *initiate* is sprinkled with blessed sand.

LEADER: Now, strengthened and purified, we

welcome you to the *inner circle* of our fellow-ship. As the child become adult, so do you come of age before us in our sacred nemeton. May the blessings of *Menw* and *Awen* be ever upon you as you enter the path of deepteachings among the *inner circle*. Blessed be!

ALL: Blessed be!

GRIMOIRE OF FON

The world around us is a magickal place. We encounter is mystical powers everyday. It flows through us at all times – and it is the essence of this unseen force that enables the wizard to function. It is the lifeforce of all living things and the very key to all physical manifestation in the material realm of form.

Many practitioners are most likely equated with the concept of *Akasha* – being directed in this work as *FON, the Forces of Nature* and *RAD, the Radiance*. Akasha is the 'quintessence' of the natural elements, sparking the motion of manifestation. Many systems have also called it the *Fifth Element*, the element of "spirit" or even the "aether."

THE VISION OF MAGICK

All systems of magick are derived from the same pure stream of *Akasha*. The elements of this work can also be incorporated in its present form into any existing 'methodology' or working tradition. And this is not limited to only 'magickal' traditions – but all spiritual and religious systems.

The essence of *Akasha* is '*light*' and all things in the matrix-existence of 'light' vibrate or radiate a degree of *Akasha* – thus making it 'exist'.

Manifestation occurs when 'light' is bent on the 'screen' to display a pattern – the slate of reality. Some modern practitioners 'realize' the 'light' that emanates from all existence as "auras." But this same energy is within and all around us in this existence – all-as-one, connected to the source of all being and existence.

* * *

Any goals, needs or desires can be achieved through the power of FON, that is the *Forces of Nature*. FON deals with the color bands of RAD energy. This is similar to what other sys-tems describe concerning auras, light shields, personal chakra energy systems, etc.

THE INNER TEMPLE

This rite is to cleanse the *inner temple* and is a preparatory ritual for FON light work.

1. Sit comfortably, hands and feet not crossing.

362

2. Visualize an atmosphere of white cleansing energy.

3. Begin inhaling it into your body.

4. Allow it to wash through you, like in the *Middle Pillar Rite*.

5. Now breathe in clear air.

6. As you breathe in clear air, see and feel it pushing out the impurities, the cleansing air is purified.

7. These impurities fall to your feet and are pushed into the ground.

8. Intone: *O Forces of White Light Energy, cleanse my Inner Temple of impurity in the name of FON. Cleanse me now. So mote it be.*

9. Visualize the white light energy returning around you.

10. Feel and see it perform a protective aura around your body, beginning with the head and moving down.

11. You are now prepared for FON work.

GOLDEN BLESSINGS

The golden light ray energy of FON can bring golden blessings. This is particularly useful for 'wealth' attraction. To attain this, you must vibrate the energy you seek to attract. As with all energetic metaphysics – like forces attract like forces. To attract a golden life, use the rays of FON to project golden light.

1. Activate the *Inner Temple*.

2. With eyes open, see golden light ray energy all around you.

3. Hold this imagery for at least three minutes and then inhale the energy.

4. Allow it to wash through your entire being.

5. Intone: *I am surrounded by the golden rays of FON – the Rays and I are one. I make them a part of myself – so mote it be.*

6. Vibrate the golden light ray energy into your auric field.

7. Practice this many times daily.

LIGHT RAYS OF WEALTH

Golden light ray energy has a significant affect on the forces of the universe. It is a unique brilliance that has the ability to attract wealth and good fortune into ones life.

1. Perform the first four steps of *Golden Blessings*.

2. Intone: *Golden Rays of FON, Golden Wealth Rays of FON, descend upon me. Make me a receiver for your Golden Rays. My desires become manifest. So mote it be.*

3. Breathe out all the hold, allowing it to become a part of your auric shield and the surrounding area.

4. Intone: *Yod-Heh-Vahv-Heh. Yeh-Hoh-Voh-El-Loh-Veh-Dah-Ahs.*

5. Feel and see the golden light ray energy becoming a part of your auric shield permanently.

6. Practice this often to strengthen the golden light shield.

YELLOW LIGHT, CLEAR MIND

The color band of yellow rays are used for mental brilliance and a clear mind. This is very useful for times when mental prowess is most critical.

1. Activate the *Inner Temple*.

2. Create an atmosphere (the surrounding room environment) of brilliant yellow light.

3. Inhale this yellow ray energy and light.

4. Fill you body up with the yellow light.

5. Intone: *O Yellow Rays of FON, Yellow Rays of Light – bring to me the riches of clear mind and wisdom. Shed onto me your Yellow Rays of strength and vitality. Fill me with your mana and bright radiance. Bless me with bright radiance. Bless me with clear wisdom and right action. So mote it be.*

6. Exhale the yellow rays of light allowing them to permeate your auric field, radiating outward into your surrounding environment.

BLUE CROWN, HEALING LIGHT

Concerning the Rays of FON, the color blue is indicative of healing – or more specifically, meta-spiritual wholeness and vitality. For thousands of years it has been used in energy work towards healing, associated in other tables of correspondence with tranquility and peace, in addition to the water element – all of which can be used to promote vibrant health. In ritual magick the color blue is usually associated with protection, which is in other words 'securing that which is already in existing good health'.

1. Activate the *Inner Temple*.

2. Create an atmosphere of azure blue.

3. Inhale this energy ray and light.

4. Fill your being with it.

5. Intone: *O Great power of FON, forces of RAD, Light Rays of Azure Blue. Heal my mind with your calming powers. Heal my body with your soothing powers. Heal my spirit with your tranquil powers. Cause all conflict in my being to cease to be. May peace be radiated from me.*

6. Feel the azure blue light ray energy coming to an apex above your head, swirling about to form a crown.

7. Exhale the azure blue light ray energy from your being and allow it to permeate your auric field and project into the surrounding area.

CIRCLE OF PROTECTION
(SPELLJAMMING)

Spelljamming is a sorcerer's process of disarming an enemy who is known to have used, or has attempted to use, magick against you. This working is one method of setting up a Circle of Protection used to deflect harmful external energies back to their source.

1. Activate the *Inner Temple*.

2. Activate a *Blue Crown of Healing Energy.*

3. Go to the eastern quarter of your nemeton and perform a process for *Casting a Circle*.

4. See the circle blazing with blue and white energy.

5. Visualize an image of your enemy standing just outside the boundary of the circle facing you.

6. Concentrate a white beam of RAD energy.

7. Concentrate this beam down on your enemy.

8. Concentrate swirling beams of white energy thrashing about inside your circle, building energy and protecting you.

9. Hold this imagery for three minutes.

10. Intone: *By the Rays of FON, the Powers of RAD, Raphael, Michael, Gabriel, Oriel – Be ye the powers around me as a I stand in the sacred center of the Holy Mandala.*

11. Address the enemy: *I refuse to allow your influence and undesirable attacks to affect me. Waste no more time and energy on me as I am protected by the Light of FON. I am secure in the Light Rays of FON – safe from you! Go! Now! So mote it be.*

12. See the enemy as becoming dissolved in white light, then disband the energies conjured in the nemeton.

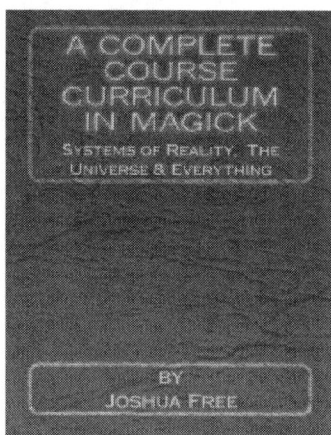

A Complete Course Curriculum in Magick
Systems of Reality, the Universe & Everything

JOSHUA FREE

The most comprehensive course in magick and metaphysics for both novice and adept alike. Prolific writer, Joshua Free has developed a revolutionary literary contribution presented in a uniquely non-linear structure that naturally adapts and evolves to a seeker's needs. Now, come initiate yourself and gain clear understanding of the harmonic unification of 'secret knowledge' that has received many labels throughout the ages: magick, occult, esoteric, pseudo-scientific and now, even quantum.

Perfect for solitary seekers and working groups. Self-paced instruction provided by a leading member of the underground occult community, available without membership and in the privacy of your own home, office or secret chamber. For the first time since its prestigious debut release in 2008, the "Great Magickal Arcanum" materials are available as an all-in-one volume!

* Easy to read - Easy to learn - Easy to use!
* Nearly *1,000* topics and subjects.
* Over *250* figures and diagrams.
* *700* oversized pages of powerful information!

- Ritual & Ceremonial Magick for Invocation & Evocation of Spirits
- The Nature of Spirits, Angels & Gods, Vampyres, Druids, Dragon Kings & Elves
- Use of Spells, Sigils, Seals and Magic Squares for Love, Money & Power
- Energy Work - Auras & Chakras, Quantum, Unified Fields and String Theory
- Prophecy, Visions, Divination & Skrying, Astrophysics, Ancient Aliens & Religious Traditions
...and much much more!

696 pages, 7.44"x9.69"

ISBN/EAN13:
1463696868 / 9781463696863

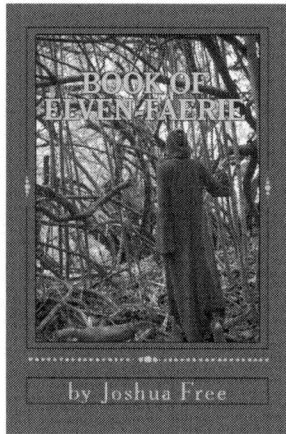

The Book of Elven-Faerie
Secrets of the Druids

JOSHUA FREE

The original underground masterpiece comes alive and available in print to the general public for the first time ever!

The Book of Elven-Faerie: Secrets of the Druids is perhaps the very genesis of the modern 'mardukite' movement, privately released by prolific writer, Joshua Free, in 2006.

Within these pages you will follow the ancient traditions of Mesopotamia (Sumerian, Babylonian) as they evolve into the mystical, mythical and societal systems of Western Europe.

Discover how the most arcane practices actually shaped the beliefs of the western world and learn how mystical lineages of modern "folk magic" can be actually traced through the evolution of human civilization on the planet - all the way back to the ancient Anunnaki and becoming the practices of the Tuatha de Dannan (Tuatha d'Anu) and other Celtic Druid tribes.

Ever popular in the underground, this book includes the complete 'Druids of the Necronom-icon' essay with its corresponding "Grimoires" of Elven-Faerie and forest magick traditions, bringing a complete Elvish Tradition to the light of the mortal world for the first time in printed history.

The Book of Elven-Faerie actually restores the historical basis of the modern "New Age" movements resulting from one Seeker's pursuits into the origins of the "Druids."

340 pages, 6"x9"

ISBN/EAN13:
1461090253 / 9781461090250

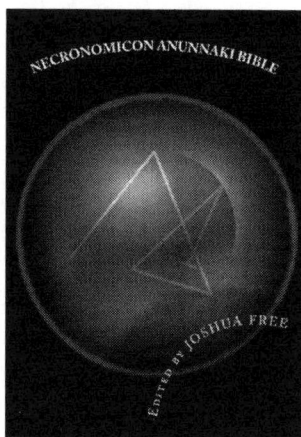

The Necronomicon Anunnaki Bible
Babylonian Mardukite Tradition

JOSHUA FREE

The Necronomicon... Sumerians... Star-Gates of Babylon... The Anunnaki... Alien Gods...

Here is the definitive work, the primary source-book of the Mardukite Chamberlains uncovered from their first active year of research and development in 2009.

'Necronomicon Anunnaki Bible' is a master-piece of Mesopotamian Mardukite Magick and Spirituality providing the most complete coll-ection of Sumerian and Babylonian accounts of human history and civilization in one book, composing in itself a 'bible' and actually proving to be the predecessor and basis of global scripture-based traditions emerging thereafter.

These are the raw underground materials have shaped the existence of man's beliefs and practices for thousands of years; right from the heart of Sumer, Babylon and Egypt! Studies into their inception as Yezidi and Zoroastrian traditions are also included!

This newly edited large-format edition presents the original "Liber N" 'Necronomicon of Joshua Free' in addition to its three companion works from 2009 that were only released to the underground and members of Mardukite Ministries.

Join the now thousands of others who have enjoyed the best of what the next generation has to offer!

What has come before is but a shadow to the realizations now capable to all self-honest Truth Seekers! Rediscover the magick and mysticism of antiquity - the most ancient traditions of Gods and Men lay here waiting to be unveiled!

440 pages, 7"x10"

ISBN/EAN13:
1461094534 / 9781461094531

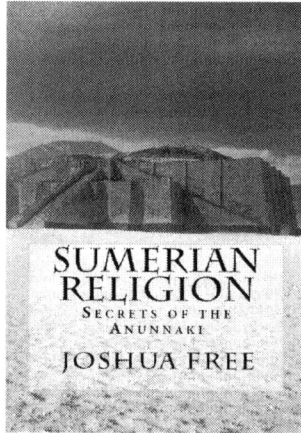

SUMERIAN RELIGION
Secrets of the Annnaki

JOSHUA FREE

The most critically acclaimed materials from the Mardukites: an account of the evolution of the Sumerian Tradition into Babylonian (and beyond) such as the modern world has never before had access to.

Developed by the next generation of seekers actively using this revival tradition in present day – not merely the presentation of dry academic renderings of obscure tablets: *Sumerian Religion* will take you on a progressive journey that is just as relevant and critical today as it was thousands of years ago – *if not more so.*

Sumerian Religion is the perfect practical companion to *all systems and traditions* as it displays the origins of human traditions on the planet, something which all can relate to. As unique as it is practical – supporting a revival tradition revealing the nature, origins and traditions connected to the "Star-Gates" of the *Anunnaki Alien Gods of Mesopotamia,* which the public contemporary society has previously only known through nearly insubstantial renderings. A clearly understood volume offering a revolutionary perspective towards understanding Life, the Universe & Everything!

234 pages, 6"x9"

ISBN/EAN13:
1461088593 / 9781461088592

MARDUKITE

ABOUT THE AUTHOR:
<u>JOSHUA FREE</u>

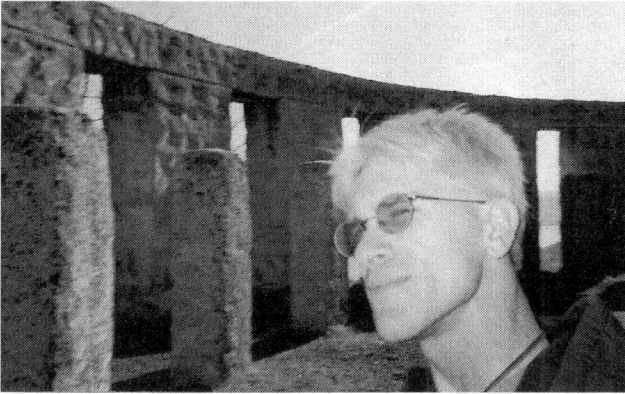

First known as "Merlyn Stone" in the 1990's, **Joshua Free** reappeared on the scene in 2008 with the launch of *Mardukite Ministries* on the Summer Solstice that year.

He is now *Archbishop-Patesi* of the *Mardukite Archdiocese of North America* and the *Mardukite Chamberlains, Nabu Maerdechai.*

His prolific writings include: *Arcanum, Book of Elven-Faerie, Sumerian Religion, Babylonian Myth & Magic, Necronomicon Anunnaki Bible,* and *The Sorcerer's Handbook of Merlyn Stone* among several others.

In 2011, he released his first novel of published fiction titled The Hybrids..

41273144R00227

Made in the USA
Middletown, DE
10 March 2017